A Family Memoir

A Family Memoir

By
LYDIA HENRICKSEN

As told to
RENATE PORE

authorHOUSE®

AuthorHouse™
1663 Liberty Drive
Bloomington, IN 47403
www.authorhouse.com
Phone: 1 (800) 839-8640

Published by AuthorHouse 11/13/2015

ISBN: 978-1-5049-4877-7 (sc)
ISBN: 978-1-5049-4878-4 (e)

Library of Congress Control Number: 2015914552

Print information available on the last page.

This book is printed on acid-free paper.

CONTENTS

Lydia Henricksen at 90

Preface by Lydia

This is a story about a family. It's about my family living in Germany through World War I and II, two of the most terrible catastrophes in human history. It's a story about struggle, sacrifice and survival. I'm writing this story for my children, grandchildren and their children so that they should know about me and where I came from.

I'm writing this story in my 90th year in Pacific Grove, California. I was born in 1925, in Giessen, Germany, in a world which few could comprehend today. The lives of my children, grandchildren and great-grandchildren are as different from mine as night is from day

When I was born, Germany was a defeated country in constant economic crisis. Many families that were prosperous before the First World War, including ours, lost everything in the cycle of inflation and depression between 1918 and 1933.

Political crises followed economic chaos. The old aristocracy lost the confidence of the people and was eventually replaced by fascism and the fanatical leadership of Adolf Hitler. I lived through the horror of World War II, when hundreds of bombs dropped from airplanes over a series of 36 raids destroyed more than 75 percent of the city where I lived. My immediate family was lucky to survive. Many others were not. In the town of Giessen more than 800 lives were lost in the bombing.

As a girl and young woman, I could barely comprehend what was happening around me. I was strong and optimistic. I survived and prospered despite all the odds. In 1953, I left Germany with my two children, Renate and Elda, and came to America to be with my new American husband, Earl Henricksen. His army career took him to Fort Ord, California, and we settled in the quiet and scenic community of Pacific Grove on the Central Coast of California.

In America, I had two more children, Ron and Barbara. I built a successful career, and eventually we had many friends and a beautiful home. But the memories of those years growing up and surviving the war in Germany have haunted me, and I don't want my story to be forgotten.

Lydia Marx Wessolek Henricksen
2015

PREFACE BY RENATE

My mother, Lydia, always wanted to tell her story. As a child and young woman, she lived through extraordinary times of terrible hardships and loss. Today she lives in Pacific Grove, California, in a lovely home surrounded by children, grandchildren, and great-grandchildren. Between her life in Germany in the 1930s and 1940s and her life in California today there could be no greater contrast. She is still young at 90 and as feisty as the young woman portrayed in this memoir.

Born in 1943, I shared much of my mother's younger life. As a young girl, I heard many of the stories she wants you to know. They left their impression on me, and I have my own memories of that time.

My mother's greatest regret is that she was denied an education. Like most Germans, Mom finished school in the eighth grade and received some secretarial training after that. She has a sharp mind and great curiosity. She is competitive and focused and would have done well in college and any profession she chose to master.

Unlike my mother, I was lucky enough to be offered every educational opportunity available, and I took them all. As a college student I was disturbed and troubled with what I learned about Germany in the Third Reich. I wanted an explanation. I wondered if my beloved grandparents and other family members were connected to the terrible human atrocities of Nazi Germany. I wondered if there was some fundamental flaw in the German character and what that meant for my own character.

My hunger for understanding led me to study history and German for more than sixteen years in college and graduate school. I earned a PhD in German history and was able to satisfy some of my need to know.

This is my mother's story, but we had similar childhood experiences, and sometimes I insert my voice into her narrative to amplify and deepen her words.

Most people who live through extraordinary times know little about who or what is deciding their fate. They are swept along in a series of events. As a student of history, however, I have the long view and want to put my mother's story in the context of the time and place in which she lived. To distinguish between her voice as the author of her story and my voice as the historian, I have added my comments in italics at the end of each chapter.

I also want my mother's descendants to know a little something about the long tradition and rich heritage from which our family comes. This tradition and heritage shaped not only her personality and view of the world but mine as well. This is especially important to understand for mother's children and grandchildren living in California and Colorado, where everything is always new and rapid change leaves little time for traditions to develop.

Renate Pore
2015

ACKNOWLEDGEMENTS

Thank you to friends and family members, who encouraged this endeavor and made helpful edits. I'm especially grateful for the good advice and encouragement of my brilliant friend, Kate Long, who talked to me about the craft of writing and encouraged me to think about how to write using different voices. My dear friend, the travel writer, Carole Terwilliger Meyers inspired me with her own touching World War II story about her father. She made many helpful suggestions and straightened me out on my use of commas and other basic grammar. My good friend, the poet, Jean Anaporte, brought her gift for words to sharpen and improve the narrative. Betty Rivard generously reviewed the final manuscript and gave me many good suggestions.

Sharon Carte sat through countless retelling of these stories and asked thoughtful questions. I thank her for her patience.

I'm also thankful to my siblings, Ron Henricksen, Barbara Beals and Elda Morris, who encouraged Mom and me to put her memories in writing and asked questions that improved the narrative. Thanks also to my niece, Lydia Beals and her son Jon, who took time to read and comment on parts of the manuscript.

My cousin-once-removed, Werner Munzert, shared his father's letter with us and provided us with a genealogy of the Munzert family. My Uncle, Adolf Marx, shared his memories of growing up in Giessen and the war years.

For details about the bombing in Giessen and eye-witness accounts, I relied on two books: *Giessen – ein Kriegsende, (1995)* and *Der Untergang des Alten Giessen (1994).* These books were a project of the Upper Hesse Historical Society and published by the Giessener Allgemeine. The books were edited by Richard Humphrey, Rolf Haaser, Meike Kross, Miriam Pagenkemper. These books are a treasure-house of detail about the impact of the war on Giessen and its inhabitants.

I regret that I am not more skilled in the art and craft of creative non-fiction. My mother's story is important not just for her children and grand-children but also because it is a very human story of strength, resilience and survival.

Renate Pore

A typical street of old Giessen

CHAPTER 1

The University City of Giessen

Lydia

I grew up in the beautiful university city of Giessen, Germany. Giessen is located in central Germany in the state of Hessen, one of sixteen states, which now make up the Federal Republic of Germany. Today Giessen has a population of about 80,000. In my day, it was probably more like 50,000.

I remember Giessen as a compact and comfortable place. We did not have, nor did we need, a car to get around. Our grocer was across the street. The bakery for bread and creamy pastries was just around the corner. The movie theater and all types of specialty shops were also nearby on the Seltersweg, one of the main thoroughfares through town.

Bars, restaurants, and the cafes where Germans liked to have their afternoon coffee and apple strudel were also a short walk away. At the tender age of 6, I walked to school with my friends and did the shopping and other chores for my mother. I never felt a sense of danger walking around our town, and sometimes my friends and I would wander blocks from home looking for adventure.

Our family lived in the Wolkengasse which was in the center of the bustling town. It was one of several narrow connecting streets between the Seltersweg and the Bahnhofstrasse, the two main thoroughfares through Giessen. In German *Wolke means cloud* and *Gasse* means a narrow street or alley. I liked the thought of living on cloud alley. In addition to our house, which was a three-story-plus-attic apartment

1

building, the Wolkengasse housed other apartments, a shoe factory, a casket maker, a bicycle shop and a seed company on the corner of the Wolkengasse and Bahnhofstrasse. My younger brother, Adolf, started his career and met his wife Irmgard there. He made a lifelong career selling seeds to the plant nurseries in Hessen. My family also had a two-story weathered barn right across the street from our apartment where we stored the hay and kept our horses, pigs, chickens, and occasionally some rabbits.

The barn with farm animals in the middle of town was a bit unusual even in my day. It was a fun place for me and my brothers. In summer, the barn had a wonderful smell of hay and animal odors and I could laze the day away reading in the hay loft.

It wasn't all fun, of course. We also had to help with the chores, carrying the slop to the pigs and feeding the chickens. On an occasional Sunday, my father would take our hard-working horse out of the barn to give rides to the boys up and down the Wolkengasse.

Karl Heinz Leuning with our horse, Sannie, and my father.
My mother is in the background

While we had a grocer across the street for the staples, we relied on the *Giessener Marktplatz* "Marketplace" for cheese, fresh fruits and vegetables. Several times a week, farmers from all over Hessen would come to the market in the city center to sell their produce. It was a fun and lively place to shop. We would walk from booth to booth comparing prices and quality. And, if we were lucky, we might get a free plum or apple.

Part of the market atmosphere was the farmers and their wives, who were very different from the residents of Giessen. German villagers dressed in their traditional costumes well into the 1950s. For the women, this meant several layers of petticoats covered by a navy blue skirt touching the top of sturdy shoes. An embroidered blouse covered by a scarf and an apron completed the outfit. On their head, some women wore a tiny hat tied under the chin. For centuries, Hessian farm wives had worn their long hair in a little bun on the top of the head, and so it was in my time.

For festivals the farmers and their wives had a fancy dress-up version of the traditional costume. These costumes were made from expensive fabrics of rich reds, blues and greens and passed down from generation to generation. They also took great pride in dressing their children in beautiful traditional costumes.

The villagers all spoke different dialects, depending on the village from which they came. These dialects were impossible for me to understand. The people of Giessen had their regional accent, which today still identifies me as coming from Hessen to Germans familiar with the various regional accents. The Giessener dialect, however, is still based on standard German taught in schools and is the norm for media speech, whereas the village dialects are a different language more closely aligned with Swedish, Danish and English. Today, the older people in Hessen's villages continue to cultivate their dialect, which makes it hard for an outsider to understand. Everyone learns standard German in school but, when speaking with each other, villagers may lapse into the old dialect.

When I was growing up, life in the city was very different from life in the country, and life among the city's university community and other elites was different from our life on the Wolkengasse. Growing up with such rich and varied traditions shaped my view of the world and respect for people of all kinds.

Giessen had other charms that I remember as a child. There was the botanical garden in the middle of town, a beautiful peaceful place with an enormous green-house filled with exotic ferns and other tropical plants. Nearby was the *Stadt Theater* or city theater with two huge and half-naked female figures on top holding the masks of comedy and tragedy. The Stadt Theater, is a beautiful classical structure, commissioned by the city fathers in 1906. Originally, the building included a triumphant hero with his horse and chariot between the two female figures. But he was melted down during World War I to support the war effort. Before the age of television, the beautiful buildings in Giessen and the images which adorned them made a big impression on me promising there was a world grander than what I knew from the Wolkengasse.

The university was established in Giessen as early as 1607, making it one of the oldest universities in Germany. Its early focus was on the natural sciences. Having started with just a few hundred students, today's university, called the Justus Liebig University Giessen, has more than 24,000 students and is an important part of the city life and economy.

The university is named for its most important professor, Justus von Liebig, the founder of modern agricultural chemistry and inventor of artificial fertilizer. Even as a child, I knew professor von Liebig was an important person because he had a street named after him and an imposing bust was mounted in front of the laboratory where he did his work. The University of Giessen was also home to 19th century professor of physics, Wilhelm Roentgen, who discovered X-Rays. A memorial to Roentgen depicting X-Rays as metal rods going through rock stands near the Stadt Theater. There was much to see in Giessen that could stimulate the mind of an imaginative child.

The city of Giessen originated in 1152 when Count Wilhelm von Gleiberg established a moated fortress overlooking the beautiful and fertile Lahn River Valley. Today, the ruins of von Gleiberg's fortress still dominate the landscape. In my time, the restaurant on the Gleiberg was a popular destination for families to spend a Sunday afternoon drinking coffee or having a beer. Today, the Gleiberg remains a popular spot to enjoy German food or a beer in the restaurant or the terrace. If visitors are really lucky, a wedding party might be scheduled for the day and they can enjoy the music and the fun.

From the Gleiberg, one can see out over the Lahn and the fertile valley it has carved. The Lahn winds its way for 152 miles through Hessen and beyond, through a rich and beautiful countryside, and empties into mighty father Rhine at Lahnstein near Koblenz. The Rhine is Europe's second longest river, flowing for 760 miles from the Swiss Alps to the North Sea, and creating the border between Switzerland, France and Germany. The Rhine is also the source of many legends and stories, including Richard Wagner's magnificent series of operas, *the Ring of the Niebelungen*, where siren-like Rhine maidens mingle with dwarfs, dragons, heroes and gods to spin out a heroic tale of love, lust, and betrayal.

Another famous Rhine legend is the Lorelei. It is said, in long forgotten times, a beautiful maiden sat on a cliff overlooking the Rhine to comb her golden hair and sing a plaintiff song, which lured sailors to their death on the shoals below. If you listen carefully, they say, you can still hear the echoes of her song.

The Lahn flows through the middle of Giessen, dividing the town into north and south. For me and my family, the Lahn was a place of summer recreation where we went for sunbathing, swimming and playing around. All along the Lahn, German families cultivated small gardens where they grew flowers and vegetables and spent sunny Sunday afternoons enjoying their little bit of nature.

Until World War II, Giessen was a charming medieval town with narrow streets and beautiful buildings. One such famous building housed the *Engel Apotheke*. A golden angel blowing a horn crowned the four-story post and beam building that had a pharmacy on the ground floor and apartments above. The Engel Apotheke was destroyed in the war and never rebuilt. A sad loss.

The old Giessen where I grew up was almost totally destroyed by Allied bombing in December 1944. Some important buildings such as the Stadt Theater were restored to their former splendor, but much of old Giessen was torn down to make way for a modern city of large department stores. Our house and most the Wolkengasse escaped destruction by Allied bombing, but were taken by the city fathers to build their vision of a new Giessen. Many other heavily bombed German cities decided on a different course and preserved their old character. It makes me sad that Giessen chose not to do so.

Renate

A generation later, I grew up in Giessen much as my mother described it, although by then most buildings were either totally or partially destroyed. Still, we both grew up in the same house with the same memories of the barn and farm animals. Like my mother, I went to the Marktplatz and did the shopping for my grandmother. From as young as age 5, I walked almost daily to the corner bakery to get bread. I also walked to school with friends from the very first day of the first grade. I loved the Marktplatz as a fun place where I might be given or snitch a piece of fruit that had fallen from the stand.

With my playmates, I roamed far and wide around Giessen exploring the ruins of the old city. We sorted through the rubble to search for bits of china or pieces of metal, which we sold to the junk dealer for a few pfennigs to buy candy. It was dangerous play because there was always the possibility of unexploded ordinance or falling off steps that led to nowhere. The newspapers regularly reported such events but, fortunately, it didn't happen to any of us. I doubt that mother and grandmother ever knew what I was up to.

I had the good luck of seeing several magical performances in the Stadt Theater. I will never forget a production of Hansel and Gretel that scared and thrilled me. On a visit to the Maerchenland or fairy tale land in the 1950s, I was careful to keep my distance from the witch.

I wondered about the lives of famous professors, who did their research in Giessen and changed the world with their inventions. I found solace in the peaceful atmosphere of the botanical gardens. Sunday excursions with my mother and grandparents to the Gleiberg or other destinations outside the city were always joyfully anticipated events. Even from 1945 to 1953, when the Germans had to rebuild their lives after the devastation of war, family life continued as before, and for me Giessen was a good and fun place to grow up.

Today Giessen is a bustling modern city. Some of the old buildings have been restored, but like my mother, I too am sad that the Wolkengasse was taken to become a commercial center and most of the charm of the old city has been lost forever.

CHAPTER 2

My Grandparents

Lydia

August Marx and Anna Uhl

My paternal grandparents were August Marx, Sr. and Anna Marx, born Anna Uhl. I don't know much about my father's side of the family. The oldest Marx family member I knew was my grandfather August Marx, Sr. He was born in 1876 and died in 1928, when I was only three years old. I have no real recollection of him. When I was a baby, he lived on the first floor of our apartment house and we lived in the attic. My mother says that when he leaned out the door and called up to me, I would slide in great excitement on my backside down the forty or so steps to be gathered in his arms.

My grandfather's children were all boys. I was the first girl in the family and the first grandchild. They said I was the light of his life. As for me, I don't remember much except the feeling that I was cherished by both my paternal and maternal grandfathers.

My grandfather Marx's life had not been easy. As best we know, the Marx family prospered in the area around Giessen for generations. When my grandfather was born in 1876, it was a good time in in Germany. He established a prosperous transport business in Giessen. At the same time, the Marx family continued a rural life in the middle of the growing town.

He owned three work horses, which he used to transport materials from the railway station to the fledging businesses and manufacturing plants in Giessen. The horses were housed in a barn built onto a small low-storied cottage where grandfather August and his brother Heinrich grew up. In addition to the horses, the barn housed pigs and chickens that kept the family well-fed.

We know Grandfather Marx was prosperous because in 1911, at age 36, he built a handsome four-story brick house on a large lot across the street from the cottage and the barn. This house was at Wolkengasse 18, where my brothers and I grew up and where two of my four children were born.

The house in the Wolkengasse built by
My grandfather August Marx, Sr. around 1911. My parents
lived there until 1963, when my father died. Members of the
Marx family are looking out of the first floor windows.

Wolkengasse 18 was a special place. It was in the heart of a growing city with many amenities such as movie theaters, elegant cafes, and bath houses. Behind our house at Wolkengasse 18 was a beautiful garden full of fruit trees and berries that was owned by a prosperous family on the Bahnhofstrasse. As children, we played in this garden and helped ourselves to apples, pears, and plums that had fallen on the ground. During World War II, the garden housed a shelter where neighbors took refuge from the bombing.

By the time I was 10, a high brick wall separated our property from the garden and it became harder to gather fruit. But, by then, we had our own little garden right behind the house, where we grew our own fruits and vegetables.

Next to our house was a large yard where grandfather Marx kept his wagons. As children, we enjoyed climbing on the wagons and taking imaginary trips around the countryside. In the fall, we had great romps outside of town, where my father and grandfather had rented acreage to grow hay to feed the horses and potatoes to feed the family. After a long hot day of cutting hay, the adults would all pitch in to stack it high on the wagon. I'll never forget the delight of sitting high on the sweet-smelling hay, like a queen surveying her kingdom, and the comforting sounds of *gallop, gallop, gallop* as our steady horse pulled us back to the Wolkengasse. We had the best of both worlds - the amenities of a city and the remnants of an idyllic rural life.

Grandpa August's younger brother was Heinrich Marx. He was the owner of a glazier and window framing business in the Loewengasse just around the corner from us. Great-uncle Heinrich was a good craftsman and his wife, Lily, was a gifted businesswoman. Together they made the business prosper. Great-uncle Heinrich and Great-aunt Lily had no children of their own, and they showered affection and gifts on me and my brothers. They were always especially generous to us at holiday times. As a child I loved to visit the bustling glazier shop with its sweet smell of wood shavings and the whirr of the machines cutting glass.

My grandfather August Marx married three times and had four sons, two by the first wife, Anna, and one each by wife number two and three. He married Anna in 1902, at the beginning of a new century full of promise for a united and prosperous Germany. In those years, the young Marx family was doing well.

The good and prosperous times, however, did not last. In 1914, when August Marx, Sr. was 38, his prosperous business and comfortable family life were sucked into the great catastrophe that was World War I. About that time his wife, Anna, died probably of heart disease, and he was left to raise two young boys, my father, August Jr. age 11, and Christian, age 8. He remarried quickly and by 1915 had a third son, Heinrich. I don't know what happened to Grandpa Marx during World War I, 1914 – 1918. He was probably too old to serve on the front lines but his horses and wagons were useful for the German war effort and he most likely put himself and them at the service of the German military.

We know he served in the military because many years later in 1939, at age 14, I interviewed for a job with the German military procurement division in Giessen. The elderly colonel, the career officer in charge, looked at me and saw a skinny 14-year-old girl. He said I was too young to work there. "I'm not running a kindergarten here. But as he looked at my application, he changed his attitude. "I served in World War I with an August Marx," he said thoughtfully. "Was he your grandfather?" I told him the man he remembered was indeed my grandfather. He lightened up and said, "Your grandfather was one of the most able and loyal men I have ever met. If you are at all like him, you can have the job." I was hired on the spot and stayed for five years, typing, answering the phone and keeping track of military supplies. Then as now, it helps to know the right people.

I grew fond of the old colonel and over the five years that I worked for him, I learned a lot. He had a stern Prussian sense of order, which he instilled in me. When I would rush into work breathlessly at 8 AM, he would remind me of the virtue of punctuality and say, *"Zehn Minuten vor der Zeit ist des Deutschen Puenktlichkeit."* "Punctuality for a German means showing up ten minutes before the scheduled time." Even today, I make sure that I always arrive early for an appointment. The old colonel also had his softer side. He and his wife had no children, and when I married my first husband, Heinz Wessolek in 1944, he cut every rose in his garden to give me a bridal bouquet.

When Grandpa August Marx set out to do his duty in World War I, he left behind a new wife, Ida, three sons, and a handsome new house on the Wolkengasse. By 1918, Germany had lost the war. Soon after, Ida died. Grandpa Marx married a third time and had one more son, Fritz.

In Germany in those days it was expected that sons would follow in their father's footsteps. As the eldest son, my father, started working in the transport business at a young age. His younger brother, Christian, was apprenticed by Great-uncle Heinrich in the glazier business. When, in 1928, Grandpa August died at age 52, my father, August, Jr., inherited the business.

My father and mother also inherited the care of the younger brothers –Heinrich, age 13, and Fritz, age 8. Heinrich, known as Uncle Heini to me, was the black sheep of the family. He was a typical teenager, who regularly got into trouble and made my mother's life difficult. He left Giessen as a young man, married twice, and I did not see him again until my father's funeral in 1963 when he picked me up at the Frankfurt airport and drove me to Giessen in his imposing black Mercedes – a sure sign of success in Germany and elsewhere. My other Uncle, Fritz, died of tuberculosis at age 17.

My father was a very intelligent man. He was especially good in math and could figure complex numbers in his head without paper or pencil. In another time or another place, I believe he would have been a very successful business man. As it was, he was trying to make a living in Germany in the 1920s. This was a time of mass unemployment, starvation, hyperinflation, economic chaos, and political turmoil; it would eventually lead to the radical politics of Adolf Hitler and his National Socialist Party (Nazis).

While my father did not prosper, our family was better off than many others. He made a living with his horse and wagon and supplemented the family income by raising potatoes and farm animals. At one point he was doing well enough to buy a truck. With the advent of World War II in 1939, my father was inducted into the military and the horses, wagons and truck were confiscated. Because of his math and business skills, my father was sent to France to become the procurer for a German military hospital. This job was to benefit our family as French farmers sent packages of food to the *Wolkengasse* to win favorable treatment from my father.

When he returned from the war in 1945, he had to start from scratch. He also seemed to have lost his ambition and his edge. He was happy to be alive, have his family and carry on in the best way he knew. Thanks to the money that my new husband and I had saved, he was able to buy a new horse and wagon and become a contractor for the city, which was digging its way out of the rubble that had been Giessen.

Renate

In many ways my family's fortunes and misfortunes mirrored that of Germany as a whole. When the various small German states, duchies and territories were unified for the first time in 1871, it ushered in a time of prosperity for the new nation state. Among other things, unification allowed for rapid industrialization that changed the German states from an agrarian to an industrial society.

It also allowed the new German nation to compete with Great Britain, France and Italy in the hunt for empire. With their new industrial power, the European nations sent their superior armies and navies around the world to subjugate the people of Africa and Asia. Their rivalry over empire would eventually lead them to confront each other in a great world war. In 1914, Germany and the Austro-Hungarian Empire went to war against France, England, Russia and eventually the USA.

World War I ended with the surrender of Germany in 1918. Germany lost its empire and of its territory west of the Rhine River (Alsace-Lorraine) and was forced to pay heavy reparations to the victorious powers. If World War I was difficult for those Germans who served on the front lines, the post-war years would be as bad or worse for the average German, as the nation was wracked by revolution and economic ruin.

In the Downfall of Money (2014), the historian, Frederick Taylor, describes the impact of those years on *the average German as money lost its value and the cost of living soared. "Millions lost everything they had when it took a barrel of paper money to buy a loaf of bread. In one three month period in 1921, the cost of living increased by 40 percent, potatoes cost 1 mark a kilo on February 5 and almost doubled at 9 marks by June. A contemporary observer described German children showing symptoms of under-feeding and malnutrition. There was also a lack of soap - a huge problem for a people who prided themselves on their cleanliness." (Frederick Taylor, The Downfall of Money, New York, 2013.)*

Karl Eduard Munzert and Margarethe Rechts

My maternal grandparents were not anything like the Marx family. They were working class, and lived from pay check to pay check in cramped quarters. They had no gardens, potato fields or farm animals. They raised their six children in a small apartment in row houses provided by their employer. Unlike the Marx family, which had lived for generations around Giessen, the Munzerts were relative newcomers. My mother always told me that her family had been miners who came to Hessen from the French region of Alsace-Lorraine. I was lucky to know both my grandfather, Carl Eduard Munzert, and grandmother, Margarethe. Grandfather Munzert lived until 1940, when I was 15 and grandmother Munzert lived until the late 1940s.

My maternal grandparents,
Karl Eduard and Margarethe Munzert
around 1940

My grandfather Carl Eduard was born in 1878 and married Margarethe Rechts in 1899. On their marriage license he was described as a miner,most likely an iron miner, and she as a housemaid. They raised their family in Lollar, a small village about 10 miles from Giessen. Grandfather Munzert worked in the ironworks of the family firm of Buderus, established by Johann Wilhelm Buderus in 1731. The Buderus firm still operates in Lollar, and descendants of the Munzerts continued to work there until recent times. Today Buderus is no longer a family firm, but instead an international corporation continuing to provide jobs in the area.

My grandparents Munzert had six children: Karl (1900), Elizabeth (1902), my mother, Margarete (1904), Albert (1907), Willie (1912), and Ernst (1915). My maternal grandparents were wonderful people. Although they had little money, they made the best of it. Food was simple but there was enough. Despite a day of hard labor, Grandpa Munzert always came home cheerful, cleaned up from the day's dirty work, and was ready to enjoy family life. I have very fond memories of him as a person of infinite kindness, patience and fun. He spent many hours reading to me and telling me stories. The Munzerts were a very musical family. They spent most evenings playing music and singing. When money was tight, the boys in the family formed a band and made extra change serenading the neighbors. During the war, Uncle Ernst joined a military band.

My uncle Karl was the oldest son. He became dissatisfied with country life and left Lollar to try his fortune in the big city. He married but left his wife and children – a disgraceful thing for a German family. We never heard from him again.

Many years later, I was told by his sons, that Uncle Karl met a bad end while working on the cathedral in Cologne, perhaps as a stone or iron worker. Towards the end of the war, he was overheard making disparaging remarks about the Nazis and predicting a quick defeat for Germany. This was treasonous talk. The authorities took him to Theresienstadt, a concentration camp in what is now the Czech Republic and there he was executed. At the time we knew nothing about Theresienstadt or other concentration camps and the horrors inflicted by the Nazis on the Jews, mentally incompetent people, homosexuals, and anyone else the Nazi Regime did not deem fit for the new Germany they were creating.

Uncle Albert's wedding to Aunt Anna. I'm in the front row third
from the right. My grandparents Munzert are behind me.
Uncle Albert was killed in the war.

My Uncle Albert was an engineer and the most educated member of the family. He was killed in World War II. Before he left, never to return, he married Aunt Anna and had a son, Reinhold. He also built a charming little house set in a large meadow filled with daisies and mustard flowers. My mother, brother Adolf, and I spent many days with Aunt Anna as refugees from the bombing in Giessen. We never knew when, where or how Uncle Albert died. My grandparents lost two sons because of the war and a third son, Willie, was critically wounded but survived. His terrible war time experiences haunted him forever.

Uncle Willie lived until 1983. He built his house in Lollar, raised a family, and after the war, went to work for the American military. His house is one of those solid German houses built to stand for centuries. It is in a charming location, up on a hill and on the edge of a dense and dark pine forest. A large garden in front of the house gave the family plenty of vegetables and fruits. Uncle Willie's son, Werner stayed in the house, married and raised his two children there. Cousin Werner and his wife, Beate, continue to live in the house on the forest. Uncle Willie was the only family member who ever left a written record of his war experiences. He wanted his children to know something about what he had endured. I find his letter extremely touching and have translated an edited version and included it in this memoir. After he wrote the letter, Uncle Willie tucked it away. When my cousin Werner discovered it during a renovation of the house, he tried to talk to his father about it. But Uncle Willie refused, saying it brought back too many images and memories he could not endure. Werner speculates that Uncle Willie suffered from post-traumatic stress syndrome, an ailment not spoken of during those years, but now only too familiar to us as a result of the American wars in Afghanistan and Iraq.

Uncle Ernst, the youngest boy in the family, joined the air force and became the leader in the air force band. He survived the war, moved to Frankfurt and married Aunt Lotte. Sad over the fact that Aunt Lotte had not conceived, they adopted a child during the war.

Two years later when the war ended, the biological mother came and took the child away. The family was traumatized. Soon after losing her adopted son, Aunt Lotte got pregnant with my cousin Lydia, and then again with cousin Heidi. Uncle Ernst worked for the German automaker, Opel, in Frankfurt and made a good living.

The girls in the family were my mother, Margarete, known as Gretchen, and Elizabeth, known as Gotchen. Gretchen and Gotchen aspired to be good German housewives. The Nazis defined the realm of the good German woman as that of the three Ks - *Kinder, Kueche, Kirche*, "children, kitchen, church." If my mother or aunt Gotchen ever aspired to anything else, they never told me. Gotchen married and raised three children in a tiny cottage on the main road through Mainzlar, a small village a few miles from Lollar. I remember her as a simple German farm woman. She was generous and hard-working. She lost one daughter, Lottie, to tuberculosis. A son, Armin, came back from the war in Africa but was never quite normal again because of the trauma he experienced. He never told me what he experienced in Africa. A third daughter, Gerta, lived to a ripe old age in the same house where she had been raised and left behind children and grandchildren who are still living and prospering in the area. Few in our family ever ventured far from home. Children and grandchildren usually stayed in the same town or not far away. It was not unusual for two or three generations to share the same roof.

Unlike Gotchen, my mother, Gretchen, was refined. Always careful about her looks, she had her hair done and was immaculate in her dress. She did not have much education but liked to read, and when she was not cooking or cleaning, she could be found reading the romance novellas favored by German women in those days. The novellas were typically in paperback, and were 50 to 100 pages long with colorful covers of beautiful women and handsome men in an idyllic setting. Like the romance novels of our day, the stories were about idealized love, loss and surrender.

Two of her favorite authors were the wildly popular and prolific Hedwig Courths Mahler and Ludwig Ganghofer. These novels were an escape from her every-day-life of cleaning, cooking and washing, with an occasional Sunday lemonade. She was satisfied with that. Neither Aunt Gotchen nor my mother ever worked outside the house after they married. They would not have dreamed of it. In any case, managing a household was a full-time job in those days without refrigerators, washing machines or dryers. They had no central heat. They cooked the family meals on wood-or- coal burning stoves and had gardens and orchards to plant and harvest. Shopping was a daily chore.

My mother's confirmation photo at age 14.

Renate

My grandmother always told me that the Munzerts had been Huegenots, who came from French Alsace-Lorraine in the 18th century. As a student of Reformation history, I found it interesting that the lives of my ancestors were impacted by the religious conflicts of the Reformation. Our family was Protestant, not out of any conscious decision or choice but merely because our ancestors were Protestant. Our birth, marriage and death certificates all declare us as evangelisch *"protestant"* and so we were.

I wonder, however, if the Munzert's of the 16th and 17th centuries had made a conscious choice to follow the Protestant reformers, which put them at odds with the rulers of France. The Catholic rulers of France were extremely hostile to Protestant movements and there were frequent bloodlettings. The most famous of these is the Saint Bartholomew's Day massacre on August 24, 1572, when Protestant leaders who had been invited to Paris were roused out of bed in the middle of the night and slaughtered by their Catholic hosts. The St. Bartholomew's Day massacre set off an orgy of killing where tens of thousands of Huegenots were killed all over France.

Just across the Rhine River, Protestants and Catholics lived together more peacefully. Frederick the Great, the enlightened 18th century ruler of Prussia, believed in religious toleration and encouraged oppressed religious minorities from France and elsewhere to move across the Rhine River and into Prussia. One of those Munzerts, an iron worker, took up Frederick's invitation and left France around 1800 to find work in the iron mines of Germany. He never made it all the way to Prussia but stayed in Hessen, where he married Maria Katharina Floecker and raised a family.

In reflecting on our family history, I am struck by how the great events of the day shaped the lives of individual families. As Americans we like to think we are more or less in control of our lives. The influential British poet, William Ernest Hensley, expresses this sentiment in his poem, "Invictus." He writes: "I am the master of my faith, the captain of my soul." But, it seems to me, we are always just tossed around on the sea of chance called history.

August Marx and Margarete Munzert

In 1923, on one of his trips delivering goods to the countryside, my father August Marx, met 19-year-old Gretchen Munzert. She was working in the country store where the goods were being delivered. She was shy and pretty. He was handsome and came from a more sophisticated world.

I imagine their romance began soon after the first meeting. It was a weekend romance. He spent the week working for his father's firm in Giessen and then walked, or maybe drove, his horse and wagon to pick up Gretchen on the weekends. They enjoyed the numerous festivals of German country life featuring lots of music, dancing, beer and pretzels. Gretchen's brothers probably played at these festivals, and maybe she got up and sang with them.

In those years of mass unemployment, inflation, and national misery, young August must have been a good catch with a family business and steady work. From a working class family that never owned anything and spent their lives in a cramped apartment owned by their employer, my mother moved into the Marx family, which owned a business, work animals, and an apartment building.

They married on Christmas in 1924, and I was born March 8 of the following year in my grandparents' apartment in Lollar. My mother had a very difficult delivery. When I was finally born after many hours of labor, I weighed only three pounds. There were no incubators or medical care. It must have been quite a worry for the young couple and my grandparents. They did the best they could, swaddling me in soft cotton and tucking me in a warm drawer safe from the cold of the drafty row house. My rocky start in life had no lasting effects. I grew up strong and healthy.

My first months were spent with my mother and grandparents in their small apartment. They lived there until my grandfather Munzert died in 1940, and Grandma Munzert had to leave her apartment to make room for a new generation of workers. She moved into an attic apartment on the main thoroughfare running through Lollar. She lived there long enough to experience the arrival of the American troops and had her own little adventure with the occupation. More of that later.

By the summer of 1925, my father, August Marx, brought his young family to Giessen to move into an attic apartment in his father's house at *Wolkengasse* 18. When Grandpa Marx's third wife died, my mother was expected to help her father-in-law with housekeeping and raising the two teenage boys, Heini and Fritz. Things got worse for her as Grandpa Marx became more ill. Even though she had her own child to care for and was pregnant with her second child, Gretchen Marx would have to take charge of two households including a dying father-in-law.

When Grandpa Marx died in 1928, my parents, my new young baby, brother, Albert, and I moved from the attic to the main floor. My mother combined the two households and became caretaker of her own two children plus her two young brothers-in-law. Not only did she care for a household with few of the conveniences we know today, but she was also responsible to help out with the haying and potato seeding and harvesting.

My mother remembered these days as especially difficult for her. She believed she would be financially compensated for her labors with an inheritance; she nursed a life-long resentment because she was not. By 1928, Grandpa Marx's once prosperous business had little to leave to his heirs. After World War I, the confiscation of his assets for the War, a decade of inflation and depression took its toll. The stately house at Wolkengasse 18 was deeply mortgaged and brought little income. When my mother finally received her small inheritance upon the death of my father in 1963, she had to give up all rights to ownership in Wolkengasse 18. She gave the little money she received to her youngest son, Adolf, in return for lifelong care at his house in the village of Treis. She lived there until she died of a heart attack in 1978, at age 72.

After leaving the Wolkengasse, my mother was never happy again. Hard of hearing and rather shy, she never made any friends in Treis. She missed her social life in *the Wolkengasse* and her position as woman of the house. At age 60, she dared to make the long transatlantic flight from Frankfurt to Monterey, California, to stay with my family and me for several months. But she missed Germany and was not prepared to live out her life on the coast of California, which is about as foreign from traditional Giessen as any place you could imagine.

*My mother at age 60, about the first time she made
the transatlantic flight to Monterey, CA*

Renate

I lived with my mother's parents, my mother, and my uncles, Albert and Adolf until I was ten years old. My grandmother was a loving and devoted caretaker. My grandfather seemed stern and distant, and I was afraid of offending him. I don't recall that he ever said a mean word or disciplined me in any way, but he did beat my uncles, Albert and Adolf. I often witnessed these beatings and was horrified by them.

I never knew my great-grandparents. No one in that generation or my grandparents' generation lived to a ripe old age. The *great-grandparents died in their 50s and 60s. My grandfather died at age 60 and my grandmother at 72.*

My mother's brother, Uncle Albert, died in his 50s but left many children to carry on. Several of them married Americans and are raising their children as Americans. Uncle Adolf is in his 80s and still alive. Over the years our family has had many wonderful visits with him and his wife Irmgard, both in Germany and in California. Their only son, Reinhold, died in his forties at a prematurely young age and left two sons, Alex and Tobias, to carry on the Marx family name.

At 90, my mother has had the great good fortune to know her grandchildren and great-grandchildren. In 2015, she became a great-great grandmother for the first time.

CHAPTER 3

Growing Up in the Third Reich
1925 to 1939

Lydia

In 1933 when Adolf Hitler came to power, I was 8 years old. During the next 12 years, Germany and most of the rest of the world would be changed forever. While the historical events of 1933 through 1945 most certainly changed the course of my life, like most young people everywhere and at every time, I had little interest or understanding of the great events unfolding around me. My parents never talked politics, and as far as I know, they were indifferent to the rise of Adolf Hitler and the propaganda of the Third Reich.

The first time I became aware that something unusual was going on was after *Kristallnacht* on November 9, 1938. *Kristallnacht* means "the night of broken glass." On that night Nazi gangs made a massive coordinated attack on Jews all over Germany. They smashed windows and burnt synagogues and Jewish businesses.

I was shocked to see such destruction in Giessen. I worried about Sarah, my Jewish friend, who sat next to me in school and whose parents owned a butcher shop. She was not in school after *Kristallnacht* and never came back. We asked our teachers about it but were not given any answers.

After school, I walked to the butcher shop, where Sarah and I had often walked together. I was shocked to see that the butcher shop was gone – burned to the ground. No one knows what happened to the family.

These events were troubling, but we turned our back on them and said nothing. As children, we were expected to respect authority and not ask too many questions. Perhaps, by then, the adults and authority figures in our lives – our parents and teachers – were too afraid to question the government that sanctioned such horrible acts.

I also remember that my father, who had many Jewish clients, was told not to work with them anymore. Some of these Jewish business men were his friends. I don't know what he thought about this. Sometime after he was told he could no longer do business with Jewish people, one of his Jewish friends came to our house. He gave us a painting and said the family was leaving Giessen, and he wanted to make this a gift to our family. The painting of a bucolic rural scene hung in our living room until my father died and my mother left the Wolkengasse. Like other Jewish friends in Giessen, these people left and were never heard from again. In our family we did not discuss it. I hope they made it to a safe place.

Our own comfortable routine was not really disturbed by the events around us until 1939, when the beginning of World War II swept my father and uncles into the military, and we lost our business and income. Prior to that, we did not have a lot of money, but we had enough for a comfortable and happy family life. There was always enough to eat. My mother managed our spacious four-room apartment, and my father earned enough with his transport business to make ends meet.

While many Germans did not have enough to eat in the turbulent 1920s and 1930s, we did well because we kept on a farming tradition even while living in the middle of town. In addition to horses, pigs and chickens, we also had a hay field and a potato field outside the city limits. When it came time to harvest the potatoes, the neighbors would help out for their share of the goods. We always harvested enough potatoes to last the entire year. We had eggs and, once a year, we slaughtered a pig, which provided enough protein for a growing family.

I remember the pig being laid out on a white cloth on the dining room table. To keep the pig cool, the windows were open but the shutters were closed to keep out the light. Downstairs in the wash kitchen, my mother and the neighborhood women were busy preparing to cook the pig into sausage.

The wash kitchen was a busy and communal place, where all the women living in the three-story-plus-attic apartments did their laundry, and where the pig was made into sausage. In the fall, juicy blue plums would be washed, seeded and made into plum butter in the huge wash tub. Cutting the seed out of the plums was one of my jobs, which I didn't mind because I could eat all the plums I wanted. During plum season, we had lots of *Pflaumenkuchen* or "plum cake," still one of my favorite treats.

Our family life had a peaceful routine. When my father came home from work, he took care of the horse and unhitched it from its long day of pulling the wagon around town delivering the goods that had arrived by train. My brothers and I would often help with these chores. After a simple dinner of bread and some kind of meat or cheese, my father would sit back and smoke a cigarette. My mother would knit or read. In the winter, we sat around a warm kitchen fire and listened to the radio. We had a cousin who played for the

Frankfurt Symphony Orchestra, so we always made it a point to listen when it was featured on the radio.

In the summer and winter, when not in school, we would spend most of our time outdoors, playing until it got dark. I had a lot of friends. Winters we would go sledding. Lazy summer days we spent on the River Lahn. It was a great place for canoeing, swimming and sunbathing. I never learned to swim but enjoyed the splashing and running around on the sandy beach and laying our towels and blankets on the soft grass for sunbathing. My mother would bring large bottles of water laced with a little vinegar to quench our thirst. A little vinegar in water is a better thirst quencher than just plain water.

My younger brother, Adolf, also enjoyed these outings. One day while diving to the bottom of the river, he found a dead man. We never knew who the dead man was. As soon as he was discovered, the authorities hustled us away. That night I woke up to hear my brother walking in his sleep and screaming at the top of his lungs. It was one of those experiences he would never forget.

Play in our neighborhood often centered around a huge magnificent chestnut tree, which in the spring flowered with candelabras of colorful pink blossoms and in the fall rewarded us with shiny brown chestnuts. Opening the green prickly outer skin, we took out the fruit to make necklaces, bracelets and decorations for the Christmas tree. The tree survived the bombings of Giessen and remains one of the few reminders of the Wolkengasse before the war. As for the rest, what the Allied bombings did not destroy in 1944 and 1945, the city fathers tore down in the 1950s to make way for their idea of post-war Giessen. Today, the 100-year old tree shades a playground in the middle of the busy downtown and will be a joy for generations of children to come.

Sundays were set aside as family days. On most summer Sundays, my parents would dress in their Sunday best and with neighbors and friends head for a stroll in the woods. These strolls often ended at a cozy *Waldkaffee*, "a coffee house in the forest," or a former old monastery called the Schiffenberg. There the adults would enjoy a beer and conversation and the children drank lemonade or apple juice. Along the way, we searched for lily-of-the-valley and violets in the spring and for wild strawberries and blueberries in the summer. Before the Americans came, there were no cokes or other soft drinks.

My parents in their 20s dressed in their best clothes
for one of their Sunday walks, around 1925

We tried to scare each other with stories of wild beasts lurking in the woods. Our favorite scary beast was the *Blind Adder*, or "blind serpent." It is a common venomous snake in Germany, but as far as I know none was ever seen in those woods around Giessen. When the family was in the mood for a really long hike, we would set out for the Gleiberg, a ruined fortress dating back to the founding of Giessen in the 12th century by the von Gleibergs.

The worst thing to happen in my childhood was the death of Uncle Fritz, my father's youngest brother. I adored Fritz, who was like an older brother to me. In the summer of 1938, Fritz went away to summer camp. When he returned, he complained of a sore throat. Within a few days, all of us - Fritz, Adolf, Albert and I - came down with diphtheria. There was no medicine to treat the disease. The doctor who cared for us had little to recommend except bed rest.

For six weeks, my mother tried to keep all of us in bed and quiet. At first we were too sick to care, but as we felt better, we had a hard time tolerating the restrictions. My brothers and I began to recover, but Fritz became worse. When he became delirious and tried to jump out of the living room window, my mother could no longer manage him. He was sent to the hospital, and when he came home after several weeks, he was not much improved. Everyone could see that the big strapping 17-year-old Fritz was losing weight and growing weaker by the day.

Fritz wanted nothing more to do with hospitals and resisted further treatments with all his might. But, when he was diagnosed with tuberculosis, he had no choice. He spent his last few weeks away from the family. I never saw him again. When he died, I was heartbroken.

Other than the death of Fritz, my childhood was happy and uneventful. From the time I was six until I was 14, I walked about 20 minutes daily to the Schillerschule. It was an all-girls school. I was a good student and had the same teacher, Herr Hoffman, all 8 years. I liked him and he liked me. Before I graduated at 14, he recommended me for a scholarship and further education at a technical school, where I learned typing and shorthand and other skills to become a secretary. Herr Hoffman helped me get a scholarship so that my parents did not have to pay. Most German children finished their schooling at age 14 with the 8th grade. A select few from the upper classes went on to a Gymnasium or high school, and from that group some went on for a university education. Working class children at that time were not encouraged to aspire to the Gymnasium or a university education. To this day, the limitation on my education is what disturbs me the most about growing up in Germany. Material things have never mattered very much to me, but my desire and ambition for education never left me.

At the Schillerschule we learned history, math, religion, knitting, penmanship, German and music. My favorite subject was math. At around age 14, I also started going to confirmation school, a ritual for young Lutherans. I was confirmed in 1939, but none of that stuck with me. Our family was never very interested in religion.

My confirmation photo at age 14

I was lucky in being recommended to a technical school. My time at the technical school was a secret from my father, who did not believe in advanced education for girls. "If anyone in this family goes for more education, it will be the boys," he would pronounce. The boys, unfortunately, were not that interested in further education. My father totally subscribed to the German ideal for women as *Kinder, Kueche, Kirche*, "children, kitchen and church." I, on the other hand, had no interest in any of those things. I imagined my future as being a secretary at an international firm, where I would have a chance to travel and see the world. It would be awhile before some of my career ambitions would be fulfilled.

In the meantime, I enjoyed the company of my peers through the Third Reich's version of the Girl Scouts, *the Bund Deutscher Maedchen*, or BDM. My parents did not approve of me joining the

Bund, but I insisted. It was a lot of fun. We wore brown skirts that came just below the knee, white blouses, and a brown kerchief around the neck. We met regularly for singing and hiking. We made crafts. We did not talk politics. We greeted each other with the *Heil Hitler* salute, but that was just part of the fun.

The leaders of the *Bund Deutscher Maedchen* exposed us to many new experiences. As a group, we regularly went to performances at the grand and imposing Giessen City Theater. By the time I was 18, I had seen "The Student Prince" and "The Merry Widow." Imagine what ideas that gave me. Without the Bund, I doubt if I would have ever been exposed to such pleasures.

My brother, Adolf, also remembers those as good times. At age 10, he joined the Hitler Youth. "It was a lot of fun," he will still tell you today. "We played sports and learned to shoot. There was probably also some indoctrination into Nazi ideology, but that is not what I cared about."

We also had lots of special celebrations. Christmas, Easter and Lent were all reasons to have a good time, much of it centered around family and children. The wildest celebration was Carnival – the last festival before Lent, which ushered in a season of austerity for the faithful. Every February all of Germany would prepare for Lent with wild abandon. Think of Mardi Gras. It was like that. Parades, singing, dancing, tons of confetti, and quite a bit of public intoxication.

Children had their own Lenten celebrations. Decked out in fancy costumes, they would party at each other's homes or in one of the many cafes in Giessen. My grandmother, who was a talented seamstress, made me a different costume every year. I celebrated Carnival as Snow White, Little Red Riding Hood or some other fairy tale character. I still remember *Kreppel*, a sugary kind of fried dough, much like a doughnut, as my favorite treat of the season.

My childhood was full of fun and special events. But nothing was more special in our home in the Wolkengasse than Christmas. The preparations began in November, when my mother would get ready to start baking cookies and cakes. Because she was hard of hearing, she didn't like to go out and deal with merchants. So, I went out to get the sugar, flour, butter and colored sprinkles, which were the staples to make a variety of cookies. Some would be pressed out in the shape of stars and wreaths. Others would be squeezed out of a pastry tube. I got to help with these preparations and my reward would be licking the left over dough from the bowl.

My favorite cake at Christmas, or anytime, was the *Frankfurter Kranz*. It was baked in a Bundt pan and then sliced twice and slathered with a butter cream. Butter cream also went on top and chocolate sprinkles on top of that. Even today I can still taste that Frankfurter Kranz.

A Chrismas tradition dear to the hearts of German children was the big pieces of *Lebkuchen* or "gingerbread" that we would buy at the Christmas Market. Today Lebkuchen is still part of many German celebrations. Bought at a market, it is usually shaped as a large flat round of gingerbread or as a heart hung from a ribbon. Wrapped in plastic and covered by a glossy and colorful picture of the season, it delighted my taste and imagination. Christmas *Lebkuchen* had pictures of St. Nicholas, the Christmas angel, or a manger scene. Children would hang the *Lebkuchen* around their necks and carry it around as a kind of emergency snack. Bite in case of hunger.

Oranges and bananas, which were exotic treats for Germans, also arrived from Africa in time for the Christmas season. My mother stashed these on top of the kitchen cupboard, where little hands could not reach them.

The Christmas season filled me with anticipation and excitement. The smell of cookies and oranges filled our kitchen on the *Wolkengasse* with a divine smell. When the cookies came out of the oven, I got one or two and then my mother put them in a pillowcase and whisked them away to a secret place where they rested until the holiday celebrations.

I wasn't too old when I figured out that my mother stashed the cookies in the bottom drawer of her bedroom wardrobe. When no one was looking, I helped myself to one or two of those cookies. If my mother knew I was snitching the cookies, she never let me know. I think my father snitched cookies too.

You may think cookies in a pillowcase in a wardrobe in the bedroom is a strange way to save cookies for the holidays, but in a German home where multiple generations lived together there weren't many options for secret places. Big wardrobes had multiple functions. In addition to storing clothes and also food that you didn't want to share with everyone, it was also a great place for a kid to hide whether playing "hide and seek" or just wanting to get away from adult control. Wardrobes had locks and keys but my mother usually just left the key in the lock.

Even today a big wardrobe for clothes and bedding is a standard piece of furniture in any decent German house. This is a practical solution for generations living together for when today's living room would become tomorrow's bedroom or vice versa. Wardrobes could always be moved around, whereas closets, which define the American bedroom, are pretty much a fixed thing.

The first Christmas celebration came on the first Sunday in December, when the Advent season began. My parents always had a beautiful wreath made from fragrant freshly harvested fir bought at the Marktplatz. The wreath was decorated with red ribbons and four red candles and hung from an 18-inch pole. Towards evening on the first Advent, my father would ceremoniously light one candle. The whole family gathered around, enjoyed coffee and cookies, and sang a Christmas carol or two. The next Sunday my father lit the second candle and the ritual was repeated until Christmas Eve. These ceremonial gatherings were full of good conversation, warmth, comfort and anticipation.

In late November each year, someone would arrive with an advent calendar. The advent calendar had 24 tiny doors. From the first of December, I was allowed to open one door every morning. Behind each door was a Christmas scene. For December 24, Christmas Eve, there was a double door. Behind it was a sweet manger scene with the adoring parents, Mary and Joseph, and the Baby Jesus on a bed of straw. I was often tempted to peak behind the doors before the designated day wishing it would make Christmas come faster. After opening 23 doors, the big day finally came. When I opened the 24th, I knew it was the start of a great day. How far removed these simple pleasures are from my great-grandchildren's digital world.

When you walked into our apartment on the first floor of Wolkengasse 18, you entered a large square foyer. Four doors opened from the foyer into the apartment's living spaces. To the right was the kitchen, and toilet, and to the left, my parents' bedroom, and the living room. Straight across from the front door was another bedroom. We had a toilet but no bath in the apartment. When we wanted to bathe, we did it in a wash-tub in the kitchen. For a special treat we went to the city baths, which were a couple of short blocks away. The city baths had deep tubs and hot showers and were quite a wonderful experience.

Each room in our apartment had its own coal stove, but they were rarely heated. In the winter, pretty much everything happened in the kitchen because heating all the rooms was too expensive. No one spent much time in the living room, except to sleep on one of the two comfortable couches.

In this four-room apartment lived eight people at one time - my mother, my father, my father's three brothers, me and my two brothers. I shared the bedroom with my parents, and the boys all shared the back bedroom. It must have been crowded, but I remember only good things about it. The living room was always kept separate as a special place for gatherings with friends and neighbors. When the pig was slaughtered, the shades came down to keep the room cool and dark and the pig was laid out on the living room table until it could be made into sausage. None of this seemed the least bit strange to me.

The week before Christmas secret things began to happen in the living room. The door was locked and it became strictly off-limits to children. Oh, how I was dying to know what went on in there. When I asked my mother, she told me that we were preparing the room for the arrival of the *Christkind* or "Christ Child" on Christmas eve. The Christkind was a mystery never to be seen by any German child.

In our regional German tradition, St. Nicholas or "Santa Claus" came on December 6 to check on the children's behavior for the past year. He was usually a rough looking guy wearing mostly rags and carrying a big bag filled with candy, cookies and switches. When Nicholas arrived after supper on December 6, we were asked to appear before him and recite a poem and tell him if we had been good or bad. If a child was too rebellious to recite a poem, as my brother Albert always was, and if the parents indicated the child had not been good enough, Nicholas would hand out a switch instead of candy. With the parents' permission, there might even be a switch or two across the backside. My youngest brother Adolf and I always got the candy, but my more rebellious brother, Albert, sometimes got switches. We weren't very old when we figured out that Nicholas was nothing more than a neighbor posing as Nicholas. We had the enjoyment of sniggering behind his back figuring which neighbor was doing Nicholas duties and congratulating ourselves on our cleverness.

By December 24, St. Nicholas Day was forgotten as we prepared ourselves for a different vision. In German culture, the *Christkind* is portrayed as a beautiful angel who flies through the windows of German homes to deliver a Christmas tree, food and presents.

My mother would spend the morning of Christmas Eve cooking a big holiday meal. She usually prepared some kind of bird, usually a goose, but definitely not a turkey, which was unknown in Germany.

After the Christmas meal was served around noon, it was nap time. As he did every afternoon, my father would lie down on the sofa behind the kitchen table. He had no trouble falling asleep. For me napping was more difficult, especially on the afternoon before Christmas Eve. After what seemed like an eternity to sleep and ignore the sounds coming from the living room, I was allowed to get up. Next came the bath in an old wash tub in the kitchen. At about six o'clock, everyone dressed in their best clothes and gathered in the kitchen.

We waited in anticipation for the sound of a little bell announcing the arrival and departure of the *Christkind*. My father would then lead the procession from the kitchen, across the hall and into the living room. He ceremoniously unlocked the door and checked to see if we could come in. Oh My! What a transformation the *Christkind* had wrought. The usually cold living room was warm and aglow with candle light and a fire in the hearth. A Christmas tree, decked in splendor, stood on a mantle. Below were the gifts and lots of cookies and oranges. I was so entranced with the tree, that, at first, I didn't notice the presents. Presents were not wrapped nor were there as many as we are used to today. But there were enough and everyone usually knew who the presents were for.

My favorite gifts were books. I loved reading about the lives of young girls and women like me. Like my mother, I became an avid reader of Ludwig Ganghofer, the famous German author and playwright, who wrote romantic stories about simple, honest and competent people in idyllic Alpine villages. His books are still printed today.

Renate

My mother's experiences in the Third Reich were unique in the history of Germany. Today we look back at the Hitler Youth and the Bund Deutscher Maedchen as evil institutions designed to indoctrinate an entire generation in the sinister ideas of the Nazi movement. For the participants, however, it was an opportunity for fun and fellowship much like the Girl Scouts and Boy Scouts of today.

My mother's parents were not in favor of their children being part of the Hitler youth organizations but there was not much they could do about it.

There is not any evidence that our family took any interest in politics. The exception is my Great-aunt Flora, Great-uncle Willie's wife, who was active in the Social Democratic Women's Movement. When it was time for me to choose a dissertation topic for a Ph.D. in history, I was drawn to the politics of German Social Democracy and especially the women's movement, which was an important part of party politics starting in the 1880s.

With a Fulbright Fellowship to pay my way, I was able to travel to Germany and research the party archives on the lives and activities of the women who were activists for working class and women's rights. I was intrigued by Marie Juchacz, a country girl without much education, who made it to the top of the Social Democratic Party (SPD) hierarchy. She established the Arbeiterwohlfahrt (workers welfare organization), which used the resources of the SPD and union dues for workers and their families that needed assistance. She survived the war by escaping to England with other leaders of the SPD and eventually ended up in New York advising state and local officials about setting up welfare programs for working class people.

When Hitler came to power in 1933, the Social Democratic Party was outlawed. Its leaders fled the country, ended up in concentration camps or committed suicide.

I published my dissertation, "A Conflict of Interest: Women and German Social Democracy." As a young woman, with a feminist consciousness that had a sharp edge, I felt that German socialist women too often traded women's rights for larger working class interests. I often wish I had the time to return to Germany and research the life of Marie Juchacz, to learn how an uneducated girl from a small village became a force in a powerful social movement, that swept Germany in the 1920s and in the post-war years won many electoral victories. I like to think that Great-aunt Flora was a part of that.

Christmas in Germany was as special for me as it was for my mother. After the war when life returned to normal, I enjoyed all the things my mother did. The scary Nicholaus, the beautiful advent wreath, the cozy family times in the kitchen and the arrival of the Christkind were all special to me.

After the war, when the Americans came, they brought with them the Sears Roebuck Christmas Catalog. Filled with pictures of candies, cookies, cakes and toys, I thought it was the most marvelous thing I had ever seen. It would not be the first time that I was envious of American children. I thought they must be really lucky to have such riches. I also envied them for their central heat and the fact that they wore patent leather shoes and white ankle socks in the middle of winter. At that time, I was still wearing scratchy knitted stockings held up by a garter belt and heavy shoes that came up around the ankles.

Even though I began to understand that other kids had a lot more than I, my German Christmas was always wonderful. The first Christmas present I remember was a plastic doll carefully laid out in a baby buggy. She was dressed in a pink crochet dress and hat, made by my mother. She had a pillow, a mattress and a blanket to make her comfortable. I was thrilled and couldn't wait to parade her around the neighborhood. The next Christmas my doll got a new dress and new covers for the buggy. At later Christmases, there would be a dollhouse with furniture, more dolls and books. I also loved books. I learned my first English words from the beautifully illustrated American little golden books. And, rather than Ludwig Ganghofer, I began reading "Tom Sawyer" and "Huckleberry Finn" – the German translations, of course.

CHAPTER 4

The End of Childhood
1939 to 1944

Lydia

In 1939, at age 14 my idyllic childhood ended. The Third Reich required all girls to donate a year of service in a home while boys were required to work on a farm. My assignment was as a maid in the house of the *Buergermeister*, or mayor, of Giessen. It was considered a very good assignment, but I hated it. It was hard work, especially doing the laundry in the bathtub. Wringing out big wet bed sheets by hand was more than I could manage as a skinny 14-year old. Soon I was suffering from carpal tunnel syndrome.

The household of the *Buergermeister* was made up of him, his wife, and his young son, as well as two German officers who lived in the spare room during the week and went home to their own families on the weekend. The Frau *Buergermeister* taught me to cook, clean and take orders. It was a middle class household and much more refined than anything I had been used to.

The *Buergermeister* and his family were very nice people. Sometimes I was invited to have afternoon coffee with the family, and the *Buergermeister* would engage me in conversation about books. This was a level of conversation that I had not learned from my parents. He supported education for girls and encouraged me to continue my secretarial studies. I did this in secret until I won a city-wide contest in shorthand writing. My name appeared in the paper and my parents learned my secret. To my father's credit, he sighed and gave in. "If that's what you really want," he said, "it's ok with me." My secretarial skills would come in very handy. When the war broke out, my father was inducted into the army, and I became the breadwinner for the family.

On September 1, 1939, Germany invaded Poland, unleashing the first Blitzkrieg, "lightening war," the world had ever seen. Poland fell quickly under the onslaught. Britain and France had sworn to defend Poland, and on September 3, British Prime Minister Neville Chamberlain, along with France, declared war on Germany.

My father and uncles were almost immediately drafted into the military. Our horse and wagon, the means of my father's transport business, were taken by the government. My father was a very smart man and exceptionally good in math. The military made use of his talents by putting him in charge of purchasing in a military hospital in France. During the war, he was able to use his position to send food to his family in Giessen. His meager income as a private, however, was not enough to support my mother, me and my two brothers. To help keep the family afloat, I was allowed to leave my volunteer service with the *Buergermeister* and find a job.

My mother had this portrait taken in 1940 to
send to her husband serving in France.

My secretarial skills and my relationship to my grandfather, the
deceased August Marx, landed me a job with the German military
supply unit in Giessen. The German officer who ran the unit had
served with my grandfather Marx in World War I and remembered
him with a great respect and affection.

My wages and the small amount that my father sent home paid
for the basic necessities of life. Though food was rationed, I don't
recall ever being hungry.

I worked every day from 8 to 5 and partied most evenings. It was
war time and people lived as if there would be no tomorrow, which
was tragically true in too many instances. My father, uncles and other
authority figures, who might have reined me in, were all gone. I know

my mother worried a lot about me and also about my brother Albert, who was a wild teenager.

In 1942, at age 17, I became pregnant, and the following July, I had a baby girl, Renate. I worked until the very day that I went into labor and was back to work within a week after the delivery. The old colonel was not happy about my pregnancy, but I kept my job. In the family, there was never any question that we would keep the baby. By the time Renate was born, I had lost all track of the father. Efforts to contact his family failed. He never knew he had helped bring a new person into the world. So it was in those desperate times.

My midwife, Frau Sauter, who attended Renate's birth, lived across from *Wolkengasse* 18. She had assisted in the delivery of both my brothers and would assist in the birth of my second daughter, Elda, a few years later. She kept an eye on me and was a comforting presence throughout my pregnancy. When I was coming home from work, she would lean out of her window and ask how I was doing. Other times she would ride past on her bicycle and shout out "you're doing good." That was my prenatal care. While pregnant, I also got extra rations of food, which I shared with my family.

The birth of Renate was easy but what came next was difficult. I had a breast infection and could not breastfeed her. She was hungry and cried all night long. Frau Sauter thought babies just had to get used to being hungry sometimes and advised to let Renate cry. It's the German way. Life is tough and you might as well learn that as a baby. I followed Frau Sauter's advice, but I suspect that my mother often got up at night to give Renate a bottle.

Not long after Renate was born, a new man came into my life. Walking home from work one day, I began talking to a young German air force officer, who was stationed in Giessen learning to be a pilot. By the time his training ended four months later, we were good friends. His name was Heinz Wessolek. Heinz and I had learned the same style of shorthand. During the day, at flight school, he would take notes in shorthand, and at night I would type them. He was tall, blonde, and blue-eyed,but not very handsome. He was, however, a very nice guy.

I learned a lot about flying from the transcription of Heinz's notes and always hoped that someday, I, too, would learn how to fly. I learned other things from Heinz, which later saved my life at least twice. After Heinz left, he went to Denmark, and from there he flew missions over England. We wrote each other and became closer, and when he returned to Giessen in October 1944, we decided to marry.

Heinz had been born out of wedlock. He was the son of a woman who married into a prominent Berlin banking family, and she did not want her prosperous relations to know she had a son. She gave Heinz to her sister to raise. Heinz had good memories of his adopted family, but in many ways, he was a lost soul in search of a family of his own. When we married in October, 1944, he was happy to have an instant family with me and baby Renate. After the war, I went to Berlin to find Heinz and contact his mother but was not successful.

Heinz was an idealist. He believed in the German cause and would not desert his duty when all knew that the cause was lost. He also had a strong sense of military honor. Returning from a mission over England, he and his fellow pilots came across a crashed plane and its British pilots. As the SS, Hitler's elite guards, were about to execute the British flyers, the German airmen intervened, saying, "We are bombing England, they are bombing us. We are both doing what we are told. If we crashed in England, we would hope to be treated right and become prisoners of war." The British airmen were saved, but Heinz and his colleagues got into some trouble over that incident and spent the night in jail. I hope the British pilots made it home to their families.

While the war had been raging for almost five years, and we had endured shortages, Giessen did not experience the war first-hand until 1944. By that time, the Americans, British and French were launching a major attack from the West and the Russian army was making its way into German territories from the East. We knew nothing about what was happening. The German radio and newspapers led us to believe that victory was within Germany's grasp, and the war would soon be over. Our fathers, husbands and uncles would return and life would be normal again. But, by late 1944, the war was about to come to Giessen with a vengeance. Death and destruction would rain down from the sky, and Giessen and our lives would never be the same again.

Renate

I don't remember Heinz Wessolek or any of those early childhood experiences. Until about age 23, however, I had constant and vivid nightmares of the war. I dreamed about the bombing and running to bomb shelters. These dreams were a recurring part of my younger years. They were terrifying and stressful. I don't know if they were actual recollections or based on the stories that my family told at the dinner table.

When I married at age 22, the nightmares ended. I'm not sure why. Perhaps my new husband made me feel safe. While I still have nightmares, the nightmares of the war have never recurred.

CHAPTER 5

The War Comes to Giessen
1944-45

Lydia

Living in Giessen in 1944 and 1945, I knew very little about what was going on in the wider world. I knew we were at war and hoped it would soon be over and everything would be normal again. I had no idea we were in the midst of one of the greatest conflicts in modern history, where more than 30 nations, including all the great powers threw their military, economic and industrial might into a global war. More than 100 million combatants from all continents fought around the globe from Asia to Africa to Europe. A deadly new weapon, the airplane, erased distinctions between military and civilian enemies. Marked by mass death of civilians, including the Holocaust and the first use of nuclear weapons in combat, World War II resulted in an estimated 50 to 85 million fatalities.

In the first four years of the war in Giessen, we did not experience or know of these horrors. The war was far away. Yes, we missed our fathers, husbands and brothers. Food was rationed, but we had enough to eat and our men would be returning soon, or so we thought. The only news we received was Nazi propaganda. The war was going splendidly, the newspapers wrote, and soon all would be well and we could resume our normal lives. Hitler had a secret weapon, it was said, which he would unleash against the world at the right time. As a young woman and without another point of view, I trusted the words of the authorities.

Not until late 1944 did I begin to realize that all was not splendid. In that year, British and American planes began to appear over Giessen. Between February, 1944, and the end of March 1945, Giessen was attacked from the air 36 times. The first fire bomb was dropped on March 2, 1944, on Klein-Linden, a suburb of Giessen. It was meant to disrupt the transportation system and there was little other damage. On March 18, 1944, more bombing left five houses slightly damaged.

On March 31, 1944, a British bomber crashed near the airport, with 31 houses slightly damaged. Between March and December there would be more attacks, all causing slight damage each time. In addition to the bombs, planes would fly very low over Giessen – so low I could see the pilot - shooting at the civilian population. Every time I heard a plane, I became scared. Still, with little industry to attract enemy interest, we never expected an all-out attack on our small university town.

One sunny day I was out for some fresh air, with Renate in the baby buggy. Suddenly, I saw a shadow and the roar of a plane as it flew low over Giessen. I quickly pushed the baby buggy into a narrow alley and plastered myself against the house, careful not to cast a shadow. Heinz Wessolek had told me what to do in such an attack. He said that it was hard to see objects from the air but that gunners were trained to spot people running, and that their shadows cast a larger target.

In 1944, as food became more scarce in Giessen, I would travel to a nearby farming village to trade cigarettes for milk, bread and other staples. As a pilot, Heinz received a good supply of cigarettes.

He did not use tobacco and sent all his rations to me. You could buy anything for cigarettes; they were more valuable than money. On one such day in the spring of 1944, I took the train about 20 miles from Giessen to trade cigarettes for food in the small farming village of Allertshausen, where we had good friends.

On the way back, as the train stopped at every small village, young boys age 14 through 16 got on board. They were volunteering to go to the Western Front to dig trenches and build fortifications, which, they believed, could stop or at least slow the Allied tanks. The train took them to Giessen, from where they would be transported to the front.

By the time we approached Giessen about 100 boys had gotten on board. They were in great spirits, singing popular military songs and, looking forward to doing their duty for the Fatherland. As the train crossed a wide meadow heading into Giessen, a plane came into view, headed straight for the train, and began firing. I was terrified, but my mind was clear enough to know that my best chance at survival would be to find a low place and lie down. When the train stopped, I crawled under the train into a shallow ditch, with the cabbage, potatoes and bread I had traded for cigarettes safely tucked under me.

The boys on the train decided to make a run for the nearby woods. As they clambered down from the train and ran across the meadow, I heard the rat-a-tat-tat of the machine gun as the plane flew lower and easily picked them off. Many were killed and wounded. It was horrible. My heart pounding, I lay under the train for what seemed like hours. I never knew if any of the boys made it safely into the woods.

After the plane had exhausted its ammunition and flown away, ambulances arrived to treat the wounded, and the train continued its journey. I got home about 11:00 PM that night. My mother was waiting up for me, anxiously wondering what had happened.

In his 1986 biography, Chuck Yeager, from Charleston, West Virginia, and the first pilot to fly faster than the speed of sound, wrote, "Our seventy-five Mustangs were assigned an area of fifty miles by fifty miles inside Germany and ordered to strafe anything that moved. . . . We were ordered to commit an atrocity pure and simple. I'm certainly not proud of that strafing mission against civilians. But it is there in the record and in my memory."

I began to feel more afraid. I knew Giessen was no longer safe. We had constant air raid drills and many false alarms when bombers flew over Giessen on the way to drop their load on Frankfurt or Kassel. It was difficult to sleep. When the air-raid sirens sounded in the middle of the night, we got up, put on our clothes and got ready to go to the basement. We always kept a bag near the front door with milk and a blanket for the baby, and food for the adults, and all our important papers. In Nazi Germany you could easily be killed if you didn't have the right papers.

While we counted on the sirens to give us sufficient warning to head for shelter, we all worried about our mother. She was hard-of-hearing and could not be depended upon to hear the sirens and take refuge. This was not a problem at night when we were home, but during the day Mother took care of Renate while I worked. My brother, Adolf, was still in school and my brother, Albert, who was 16 in 1944, was rarely to be seen, after having gotten a motorcycle and an important job delivering messages to the military and local officials in and around Giessen.

When sirens started to howl in the afternoons, I had no choice but to leave my desk and head home as quickly as I could. This was allowed. But before I could hit the street for the ten-minute race home, I had to take my typewriter to the basement to keep it safe.

From March to December, 1944, we lived on a nervous edge, but we had no idea of what was yet to come. After all, we reasoned, why bomb Giessen? It was a small university town of no real importance to the war effort. Giessen was part of an important transportation system, but experience showed that the bombers were very precise in hitting their targets to disrupt transportation. They hit the tracks, and perhaps a few houses would be damaged. We did not know that by 1944, the Allied Forces had decided that Hitler and his generals would never give up in a conventional war. The war had to be brought home to the people of Germany. The civilian population had to feel the pain. As Chuck Yeager wrote in his biography, American pilots were commanded to hit anything that moved.

The Allied commands impacted my life on the night of December 2, 1944, when 60 bombers roared over Giessen for 18 minutes, dropping their bombs and causing widespread damage. On that night, my mother and I were sitting in the kitchen by candlelight. My younger brother, Adolf, had already gone to bed. Albert was off on his important business. When the sirens started announcing the approach of the bombers, we woke Adolf and hurried into the basement shelter. Albert arrived within a few moments.

In the shelter we found that Adolf and the upstairs neighbors, Frau Hain and her young daughter, Doretta, were missing. We ran upstairs to hear a panicked Frau Hain trying to unlock the door to get out. We calmly talked to Doretta to unlock the door and hurried them into the basement. As we ran down the steps to the basement,

Albert and I saw that a fire bomb lay smoldering next to our house. Without much hesitation, Albert picked up the bomb with his bare hands and threw it into the middle of the yard, where the fire could do no damage.

Albert and I then started looking for Adolf. We found him in the middle of the street, looking up at the sky and totally befuddled about what was happening. He was wearing only his pajamas. We dragged him into the shelter. He remembers how on that night he was terribly cold and afraid.

When everyone in our house was safely in the shelter, we saw that a house at the end of the Wolkengasse was on fire. Albert and I raced to the house and helped to put out the fire and rescue the people.

That night we helped other neighbors to a shelter in the neighborhood. Like Frau Hain, many people panicked and were unable to act to save themselves. A young woman carrying a dead baby came into a shelter behind our house. We knew the baby had a twin brother. The mother was in such a state that she did not want to give up the dead baby to rescue its twin. Albert and I raced to her building, bounded up the stairs, found the twin and brought him to safety.

Albert and I were amazingly calm during this danger. We looked for ways to help our neighbors and never worried about ourselves. Only later, after the danger had passed, did I fall apart.

After it was all over, my mother made coffee and gathered the neighbors into our kitchen to discuss what might come next. I decided then, that it was time to leave. The next morning Adolf, Renate and I left on the train for Lollar. My mother refused to go. She was worried about Albert and did not want to leave her apartment.

Amazingly, I found this log posted on the internet from an American pilot who dropped his bombs on Giessen that night. Here's how it looked from his point of view.

(67) 2ⁿᵈ December 1944 Target GIESSEN, Germany.
F/O J. P. Morgan (pilot) and Sgt J. A. M. Sturrock (nav).

T/o 2335. A change from the usual effort; a pin-point target bombed
from 6,000 feet. This raid was quite successful, marking being
good, and a small fire being started by concentrated bombing.
Bombing times were between 0058 and 0110 hours. Some crews
obtained a visual and reported the raid to be "Bang On"!
Broken cloud drifted over the area at about 2,500 feet. There was
slight opposition which was ineffective. MM150 landed at 0305

Giessen city center after December 1944 bombings

Another story told by my daughter, Renate, brings our family and the enemy together in a strange way. In the 1980s, Renate saw a sale on boots in the little town of Elkview near her home in Charleston, West Virginia. She drove the extra miles to get a good deal. When she purchased the boots with a check, the cashier asked to see her driver's license. He looked at her license, looked up and mentioned her birth date, saying "on that day 40 years ago, I was flying over Germany." Renate's jaw dropped. She was too surprised to say anything. Leaving the store with her new boots, she thought about weird coincidences and the absolute insanity of war.

Four days later, on December 6, 1944, they came again. This time, 250 bombers dropped their load on Giessen in 32 minutes. The real damage, however, came not just from the bombs but from the firestorm they created that raged for hours and totally destroyed the ancient inner city. It was the end of old Giessen.

Margot Graef, a resident of Giessen, described that night in a poem.

Eigentlich ist sie schon tot.
Gestorben in einer einzigen Nacht
Durch Feuer und Tosen
Mit Sturm und Geheul
Wurde sie zur Asche,

Die Stadt wie ich sie einmal kannte.
Sie war einmal schon, meine Stadt
Mit alten Fachwerkhausern,
Schmalen Strassen und engen Gassen
Voller Geborgenheir
Und pulsierendem Leben
Was hat man aus dir gemacht!
1979

She is dead
Died in a single night
In fire and wailing
A roaring storm of fire
Turned her into ashes
The city I once knew

My beautiful city
With old timbered houses
Narrow streets and close alleys
Full of a snug security
And pulsing life
What did they do to you?

More than 75 percent of the buildings in the city were destroyed, and most of the rest were severely damaged. By some miracle, the Wolkengasse was spared. Some buildings were damaged but not a single building was destroyed. Yet a few yards to the right on the Bahnhofstrasse, and to the left on the Seltersweg, there was total devastation. Heinz later explained to me that the bombers flew in a V formation and that those in the middle of the V would be spared.

Wolkengasse 18 after the December 6, 1944, bombing.
Most of the Houses on the Wolkengasse were spared.

Besides the damaged and destroyed buildings, and the infrastructure of the city,800 people died that night. There would be no water or electricity for many months, and it was a miracle that more people were not killed.

Safe in Lollar, I worried about my mother and brother. I walked to the train station where the survivors arrived walking around in a daze. "Do you know what happened in the Wolkengasse?" I asked, "have you heard anything about the Marx family?" No one knew much of anything, but they told me that the city had been destroyed and many were dead. Later that day, my mother arrived safely on the train, and I breathed a sigh of relief. Albert stayed in Giessen to do his important job.

Those that died that night included a doctor, sixteen nurses and sixteen children, who were patients in the *Giessener Kinderklinic*, "children's clinic." When the bombs started falling, they took refuge in the basement. While the basement was considered a safe place, this time the exploding bomb missed the building and fell next to it, causing an explosion in the bottom of the structure. A nurse and eyewitness, who ran to the clinic to try and save the children, saw immediately that those in the shelter were burned alive. The people of Giessen, our friends and families, wondered how the enemy could be so careless. The Children's Clinic had a big Red Cross on its roof designating it as a hospital. Was it an accident or intentional? Was it naïve of us to think, that in the middle of such madness, children or the sick would be spared?

I was not in Giessen on the night of December 6, 1944. My younger brother Adolf, Renate, and I had left after the December 3rd bombing to take refuge with relatives in Lollar, a small farming village about 10 miles away.

My mother and brother, Albert, stayed in the apartment at Wolkengasse18. The afternoon of December 6, my mother, then 40 years old, put some more coals on the fire, had a cup of tea and slice of dark German bread with sausage, and settled in for the evening. She worried about her children and grandchild, wondering if they had made it safely to Lollar. She wondered about her husband, August, from whom she had heard nothing for months. For some time now, the packages of coffee, eggs and oranges he sent from the front in the early days of the war were no longer arriving.

My father was not in combat. He was a supply sergeant for a German military hospital near Bordeaux. I never knew how my father managed to send us food from the front. Apparently he had a good relationship with the French farmers, who sent packages to the Wolkengasse in exchange for whatever favors he could do for them. In any case, the packages arrived and we were enormously grateful. I always wondered how the eggs could make it in such good shape from such a distance.

After the war, my father had only good things to say about the French. He especially admired the nurses, the first professional women he had ever worked with. What a perplexing thing is human nature that we can slaughter each other with such abandon, but on a personal level there are always deals to be made and friendships to nourish. On the other hand, my father would rant and rage against the Russians long after the war was over. And I don't know if he ever met a Russian.

Safely in Lollar on December 6, our Aunt Anna tried to make it an occasion for St. Nicholas Day. Despite the scarcity, Aunt Anna was able to cook hot chocolate and serve cookies. We didn't think much about St. Nicholas that night, we were just glad to be alive and safe.

Around 8 PM that evening, Adolf was outside looking toward Giessen. He called for us to come out and see hundreds of lights floating from the sky. He said they looked like Christmas trees. They illuminated the entire city as if it were day. It was a strange and beautiful sight. We knew the "Christmas trees" were not for our delight but our destruction.

The "Christmas trees" were dropped to illuminate the target and would be followed by bombers who would drop thousands of explosives and fire bombs onto Giessen and destroy the old city forever.

After December 6, 1944, and through the winter and spring, life was very chaotic. We moved from one place to another and relied upon the good will of relatives and friends in the villages around Giessen which had been spared by the bombing.

At Wolkengasse 18, the windows were blown out. We had no water or electricity, but the house and barn survived. My mother moved in with her sister in Mainzlar. Adolf, Renate and I left our refuge in Lollar and walked in the snow to Allertshausen to take refuge with the Rampft family. Herr Rampft served in the military with my father and had more than once offered his home as a refuge. We slept on straw on their living room floor for about three weeks. I felt a bit sorry for myself having to sleep on straw on the floor, but these kind people shared whatever they had with us, and I am eternally grateful to them.

By Christmas 1944, my mother, Adolf, Renate and I were all back together again in Mainzlar. No one knew were Albert was. To relieve the crowded conditions, Renate, my cousin Lotte, and I rented a room across the street. Later, when Lottie died of tuberculosis, we all worried about Renate. She was not a healthy child and tuberculosis was a very infectious, and in those days a deadly disease.

My new husband, Heinz Wessolek, came home for Christmas. We were saving all the money he made and talked about plans to set up our own household after the war. We all knew the war would soon be over. He told me that "Hitler's secret weapons," the jet air planes, which he was learning to fly, had been sabotaged by their own commanders to hurry the end of the war. I begged him not to go back, and the family offered to hide him in Mainzlar. Despite our entreaties, he went back to share the fate of his colleagues. I never heard from him again. Many years later, I was able to get a certificate of death, when a military colleague testified that he had seen Heinz go into a building, which was hit by explosives. He never saw him come out.

I traveled to Berlin right after the end of the war to find Heinz and try to talk to his mother. I was not able to find either one of them. For Heinz's sacrifice, I eventually got a widow's pension and financial support for Renate. I'm sure that Heinz would have been happy to know that he was helpful to us in death. I know there is something profound about his sacrifice, but as a 20-year old mother and widow, I was too busy to mourn. I was just trying to survive.

By March, 1945, the Americans had crossed the Rhine River and were heading towards Giessen. We learned that my mother's brother, Albert, died in the war, but my mother, my brothers and my baby all had survived. Things would be tough at first under the American Occupation but nothing like the horror of 1944 and early 1945. At that time, we still had no idea what happened to our father, to Heinz and other family members, but we were hopeful to see them again.

Renate

The Nazis had high hopes for the new jets and rocket planes they built to push back the Allies. By the beginning of 1945, with the Russians closing from the East and the US and Britain marching in from the West, it was clear that Germany faced a catastrophic defeat, but the Nazi leadership refused to give up hope. As late as February 28, 1945, Propaganda Minister Joseph Goebbels announced to the nation that Germany's "miracle weapon" would soon turn the tide of the war.

Adolf Hitler and Hermann Goebbels had called for a total war, where Germany would fight until there was no German left standing. They continued to demand sacrifice from the population even when all hope was lost. Attempts to assassinate Hitler and end the war met with failure. The most famous of such attempts was in July, 1944, when Count Von Staufenberg brought a bomb in his briefcase to a meeting with Hitler. He set the briefcase under the table next to the Fuehrer and left the room. When the bomb went off, the heavy table took most of the blast and Hitler escaped with minor injuries. Von Staufenberg was executed. This story is portrayed in the German American thriller, "Valkyrie," starring Tom Cruise as Staufenberg.

I could not find any documentation that the Germans sabotaged their own planes to end the war as Heinz told my mother, but if Heinz said it, then it must have been true.

In talking about the boys who met their death outside Giessen, my mother recalls them singing a popular German war song "Wir haengen unsere Wasche in den Westerwald." She thought it was a patriotic German song. In reality, the song was originally written in English to cheer on the British war effort. It was then translated into German and used to parody the enemy. The Westerwald also known as the Siegfriedline was the last defense of Germany in the West.

My mother has told me this story many times. Each time I am overwhelmed to think of high-spirited teenagers leaving the safety of their homes to build Germany's last defenses on the western front. The English song and its German parody say something profound that I can't readily express. I picture the young boys climbing on the train and singing only to be shot dead like dogs a few minutes later.

Here's the English version.

We're going to hang out the washing on the Siegfried Line.
Have you any dirty washing, mother dear?
We're gonna hang out the washing on the Siegfried Line.
'Cause the washing day is here.
Whether the weather may be wet or fine.
We'll just rub along without a care.
We're going to hang out the washing on the Siegfried Line.
If the Siegfried Line's still there.

The German answer was

Ja, mein Junge, das hast du dir gar zu leicht gedacht
mit dem großen Wäschetag am deutschen Rhein
hast du dir auch deine Hosen tüchtig vollgemacht,
brauchst du gar nicht traurig sein!
Bald seifen wir dich gründlich ein
von oben und von unten her
wenn der deutsche Waschtag wird gewesen sein,
Mensch, dann brauchst du keine Wäsche mehr!

Sing dies Liedchen mit, wer es nur immer singen mag
mit der zweiten Kriegsberichterkompanie
Bis zum Wäschetag, ja bis zum Wäschetag
In aller Herrgottsfrüh.
Mein Mädel, schenk' noch einmal ein
Und tanzt und trinkt die Gläser leer.

Denn wenn der große Waschtag wird gewesen sein
Kehr' ich heim, kehr' ich hegim übers Meer.

The English Translation

Yes, my boy
You thought that washing day on the Rhine
Would be easy
But you shit your pants
Don't be sorry about that
Because we're going to clean you up
From bottom to the top
After the washing day on the German Rhine
You won't need any more underwear

Sing this little song with me
Whoever can sing with the 2nd company
Until that washday, yes that washday
In the early morning.
My sweet girl, pour me another drink
Dance and empty your glasses
For when the great wash-day on the Rhine is over
I'll come back home, home over the wide sea.

Uncle Willie 1942

Uncle Willie's Letter

My mother's brother, Willie, was the only person in the family, who left any written recollections of the war years. I am assuming that some of his experiences in being drafted and learning to become a soldier at age 30 was much the same as my father's and other uncles. During his three years in the army, Uncle Willie was all over Europe from France to Greece to Albania, and the Ukraine. He endured terrible hardships and was wounded with a shot near the heart and through the lungs. In the Ukraine, he experienced hard winters and saw action where some of his comrades were killed. Uncle Willie never shared this letter with his wife or children nor did he ever talk about the war.

In 1977, during home renovations, my cousin Werner discovered the letter. When Werner asked his father why he had not shared the letter, uncle Willie said it brought too many vivid memories. Today, we believe that Uncle Willie and many of the other German survivors suffered from post-traumatic stress disorder (PTSD). Almost 70 years after the end of World War II, PTSD, is finally being recognized and treated.

This letter is translated and edited by Renate Pore

Lollar, 1946

My dear children,

The war has been over for a year and a half, and I want to write down some of my memories for you from my life as a soldier. I want to tell you as much as I remember, no more and no less, even though some of it is very ugly.

When war broke out with Poland in September 1939, I thought that one day I might be called to serve. I was lucky and it was not until May 18, 1942 that I was summoned to appear at army headquarters in Giessen. There were 160 of us from Hessen and Thuringen, who were drafted into the army at that time. My fellow soldiers were all good and brave men. Our officers, Backer and Rohm, were decent and outstanding men. But there were also some who were a horrendous bunch *Schweinehunde*, "pig dogs."

The life of a new recruit was hard. We got up at 6:00 in the morning and went to bed at 10:00 at night. In between we worked and marched all day with a little rest while we ate. Everything from our clothes to our hair and fingernails had to be clean and perfect. If anything was amiss, even if the company sang out of tune during

---

our daily march, there would be hell to pay. After twelve weeks of this treatment, we graduated to the next phase of our training.

I came into a company where all the officers were Schweinehunde. Discipline was harsh. When two soldiers accidentally broke something, the entire company was punished. The physical labor was so difficult that one of my fellow soldiers died from the exertion.

Life became better after basic training. In January 1943, about eight months after being called into the military, I was sent to France as part of the First Armored Division near the small village of Amiens. There was not much fighting going on in France but I was starting to feel homesick and had a horrible commander who liked to make his men suffer.

When the call came for someone to carry the stretchers with the dead and wounded, I volunteered immediately to get away from my commander. As a result I received ongoing training and became an emergency medical technician (EMT). I wasn't really cut out for this work. The first time I had to bandage a bloody finger, I shook so much that I dropped the bandage. The doctor, who was overseeing my work, laughed out-loud.

From France, I went to Greece, had more training as an EMT and ended up in Albania and the Ukraine. It was the rainy season and everything was stuck in the mud. About that time, I also learned that some of the men I had entered the army with had been killed in battle. On November 20, 1943, I saw the first sign of Russians. An ice cold shudder ran down my spine. That night I drank a lot of schnaps to calm my nerves.

The next day came my initiation into the fire storm of war. We were marching through the woods when we suddenly heard shots and exploding grenades. Five minutes later we were in the midst of battle with 500 Russians. We were so disorganized and frightened that we shot and killed our own soldiers, who were in the line of fire. That day eight died and twenty were wounded. I didn't know where to start in taking care of the wounded

The battle, the bitter cold, stress and fear made me sick and I was allowed to stay in bed for a day and a night.

Our troops and the Russians hunkered down in trenches for three weeks. The close quarters and unsanitary conditions resulted in me and the entire company coming down with hair and body lice. For some days, we were allowed to retreat to the back of the lines to wash and get clean underwear. On January 17, 1945 we went back to the front lines and experienced a big attack. We forced the Russians back and took about 50 miles of territory.

In that area, we found a German family,that was overjoyed to see German soldiers. They told us unbelievable stories of what the Russians had done to them. And so it went, on and on, with civilian and military casualties on all sides.

By spring of 1945, as the Russians advanced, the Germans were driven back. Our unit marched to the mountains of Austria, where we spent the rest of the war.

On May 8, 1945 the war ended and I became a prisoner of the Americans. On July 6, 1945 I was back in Lollar reunited with my family.

These experiences were so terrible. I hope they will never be forgotten.

Your father

CHAPTER 6

The Americans Come to Giessen
1945 - 1953

Lydia

In 1945, Giessen lay in ruins. We had no running water or electricity. The population was starving. It could have been worse. As the Soviets marched towards Germany from the East and the Allies from the West, Germany would be divided into an Eastern and Western zone. Giessen was in the Western zone and occupied by American and British forces.

At the time, I had no idea how lucky that was for me and what it would mean for my future. The Soviets were known to be very harsh on the civilian populations they conquered. They had lost millions of people and suffered enormously from the German invasion of Russia, and they wanted revenge.

Many Germans living in the Soviet-occupied lands, left everything they owned and had known and started walking to the West. Many of these refugees ended up in Giessen, creating a demand on the city's scarce resources. Their suffering and sacrifice were terrible, and it would take many years before they were fully integrated into the existing population. My future sister-in-law, Hilde, was one of these refugees.

German soldiers in the East also abandoned their posts and walked west to take their chances with the Americans rather than the Soviets. As they walked through Giessen on their way home, my mother often gave them food and a place to sleep.

While the war did not end officially until May, 1945, the fate of Germany was decided a year earlier when the Americans landed at Normandy on June 6, 1944. While the Allies experienced heavy losses, with more than 9,000 killed, their army of more than 100,000 began the inevitable push-back of the Germans.

I'm not clear what happened to my father in Bordeaux as the Allied forces liberated France. In any case, he was able to continue sending us food as late as October, 1944, when he sent ham and eggs to celebrate my wedding to Heinz Wessolek. At some point after that, he became a prisoner-of-war of the Americans.

We were ignorant of the developments in the war. We began to suspect that the German cause was lost, but Hitler and his men urged resistance to the very end. The endless propaganda, no doubt, influenced many young men, who were eager to fight for the Fatherland. I know it influenced my brother Albert, age 15, who made himself available to the German military for however they could use his services, and it probably influenced Heinz to die for the cause rather than abandon his comrades.

I often wonder how my life might have been different if Germany had surrendered earlier in 1945 or if Hitler had been assassinated. As the Soviets entered Berlin in April 1945, Hitler shot himself and the Germans were able to surrender. Had they surrendered in 1944, I would have been married to Heinz and most likely lived out my life as a pilot's wife in Germany. Hundreds of thousands would not have died.

In 1945, the Allies began crossing the Rhine River, the last obstacle before Hessen and the towns that led to Giessen and other major cities. It wasn't long before American tanks began rolling through the villages of Mainzlar and Lollar. We knew then that the war was over. I was excited to see what it was all about. Some people were afraid and hid themselves. My uncle urged me and my mother to hide in the basement, but I was more curious than scared. I picked up my baby girl and ran into the street to wave and watch the tanks roll by. It seemed like a celebration. I didn't feel threatened. They were soldiers in a different uniform, not much different from our soldiers.

For the most part it was a friendly invasion, with many Germans greeting the Americans as liberators. With the American arrival I was surprised to see a black man for the first time in my life. I wasn't sure what to make of it, but it obviously made an impression since I remember it more than 70 years later. I knew that black people lived in Africa, but it had never occurred to me that they lived in America as well.

My grandmother Munzert, whom we called Oma, had a small apartment in Lollar. One day, several Americans came and told her to get her purse and leave. They confiscated her apartment. With nothing but her purse, she walked the short distance from Lollar to Mainzlar, where my mother and I were staying.

Oma was not particularly scared or angry over the invasion of her apartment. She seemed to accept it as a small inconvenience. When the weekend came, she let us know that she needed fresh underwear and asked us to go to Lollar to pick it up. Armed with my little bit of English, my mother and I, walked boldly up to the door and let the Americans know we needed Oma's underwear. The Americans were polite, ushered us in and allowed us to go through closets and drawers to get what we needed. As we started to leave, one soldier smiled at me and handed us a box, indicating that this, too, was "for the Oma."

I was very nervous about the box. Was it something dangerous? A bomb? We opened it very carefully when we got home and were delighted to discover coffee, cheese, chocolates and other food packed as K-rations for the American troops. We had not tasted coffee or chocolates for a long time. We had a good time that afternoon. It's funny how a little thing like a cup of coffee can leave such a strong memory. It is hard for anyone in America to understand how happy one can be with a cup of coffee. A couple of weeks later, the Americans moved to their new headquarters in Giessen, and Oma was able to move back to her apartment.

There were other times when I enjoyed the kindness of Americans. When my mother moved to Mainzlar after the December 6 bombing, we moved her bedroom furniture with her. We moved her furniture at night to avoid being shot by low-flying planes. By May, 1945, my mother thought it was safe to return to her home in Giessen.

My cousin, Lottie, and I got a hand wagon from one of the local farmers. We put the bed and all the rest of the bedding on the wagon and began the 8 mile trek to Giessen. On the way, a truck full of American soldiers drove by, whistling and laughing at two young women pushing a wagon. One of the soldiers jumped off the truck and placed a box on the wagon. Again I worried. Were we going to be blown up? Again it was a box of much-needed food.

After we were all back in Giessen, we had another bit of good luck. One day a box of food arrived for us from Hackensack, New Jersey. While the American Congress was debating what to do about the Germans, ordinary citizens took action. A Lutheran congregation in New Jersey had heard about the starvation and hardships that Germans were experiencing. Members of the church were urged to send food to a central address from where it would be distributed. Among the congregation was a woman who had lived in the Wolkengasse many years earlier. She remembered my father and his brothers and addressed the box to "the Marx family in the Wolkengasse" and hoped that it would arrive.

How lucky we were that there was still a Wolkengasse and a Marx family who could receive this kindness. I wrote to thank her and she sent us several more boxes of food. When the food stopped coming, I assumed that she had died. I wish I could remember her name.

During those years after the war, our family had more resources than most. In addition to the American gifts of food, we had relatives in the country villages who shared their food with us. I was also not above going out and stealing fruit from the country orchards. At age 3, Renate was too weak to walk. The doctors said she needed fruit and sunshine. In retrospect, we know that Renate suffered from rickets, a disease in children that softens and weakens the bones, usually because of an extreme and prolonged vitamin D deficiency. I did what I could to get the fruit, and my mother made sure Renate got whatever sunshine was available. At age 72, Renate continues to thrive.

By the summer of 1945, most German prisoners of war started to return. We were hoping to hear something from my father and Heinz. On a warm July day in 1945, we were all gathered in the kitchen for our mid-day meal. Suddenly we heard a familiar voice through the kitchen window. "Is there any dinner for me?" After many months of hearing nothing from our father, not knowing if he was dead or alive, we were overjoyed to see him.

My father, who also had not heard anything about us, arrived in Giessen with other prisoners of war on the open bed of an American truck. As they approached Giessen, my father saw the terrible devastation. He didn't know if his family was dead or alive. Was there a Wolkengasse or a pile of rubble? As the truck turned a corner not far from the Wolkengasse, he jumped off to walk home. The Americans might have shot him, but thankfully they let him be. He became increasingly optimistic as he saw that the Wolkengasse was damaged but not destroyed. His house still stood and when he walked up to the window, he saw his whole family for the first time in many years.

My parents and brother Adolf in the late 1940s

Full of optimism, I expected that Heinz would suddenly appear like that in the not-too-distant future. Heinz and I had saved money and planned for our life after the war. We were looking forward to a normal and comfortable life together.

Our hopes would not be realized. I never heard from Heinz again after he left in early January 1945, and much of the money that we had so carefully saved was stolen. I gave the rest to my father so that he could start his business again from scratch.

For all the good things that Americans did for us, there was also a darker side. My father had arranged to buy a horse and wagon. I went to the bank to get the cash to pay for them the next day. I carefully put the large amount of money into a blue purse and hid it in the living room buffet.

That evening the Americans came around to inspect the neighborhood. These inspections were to find guns and other weapons that Germans were not allowed to have. It was routine that everyone would leave the apartment while the Americans searched wherever they liked.

After the Americans left, I discovered the money was missing. The loss of the money still hurts. My mind still clearly sees the middle drawer of the buffet where the purse had been hidden. We reported the theft to the American authorities. They found and returned the wallet but the money was gone. The rest of the money I had in the bank went to pay for my father's business.

After my mother, brother, Renate and I returned to the Wolkengasse in May, 1945, I got a job with the American Red Cross as a bookkeeper. Besides extra money for the family, the job had the added benefit of free doughnuts. The American Red Cross provided a comfortable place for American soldiers. It was a place to relax, read the paper, call home and have coffee and fresh doughnuts. Doughnuts left over could be taken home by the staff. To this day, my youngest brother, Adolf, still talks about what those doughnuts meant for him.

Another benefit of working for the Red Cross was that we got to party with the soldiers who came there to relax. At one such party, an airman pulled out a handkerchief embroidered with a map of Giessen. "I got this in memory for the bombing missions over Giessen" he bragged to the group of girls gathered around him. What a jerk. I was so outraged, I reached out and slapped him. Lucky for me, the other soldiers dragged him away before he could react.

Despite all the advantages of the Red Cross, I disliked the man, who was in charge and soon started looking for greener pastures. By the end of 1945, I had found a job as a bookkeeper with the American Post Exchange (PX).

In 1946, I met the 22- year-old Corporal Earl Henricksen, who would be my second husband until he died in 1992, at age 68. Earl had joined the army at age 17 and served the war years in the Pacific as a guard at a prisoner-of-war camp. He had married at a young age and had a daughter named Bonnie Lou. The marriage was not a good one and when his tour of duty expired, he re-enlisted rather than go back to his wife and daughter.

I met Earl selling cigarettes on the Wolkengasse. My father heard that an American was selling cigarettes and sent me out to buy some, thinking I could use my feminine charms to get a good deal. After I bought the cigarettes for my father, Earl invited me to an American bar for beer and dancing.

One date led to another. Earl brought food and cigarettes for the family and became a welcome guest. He learned some German and I became more proficient in English. We spent many evenings at the movies watching the singing cowboys, Roy Rogers and Gene Autry, that the Americans loved so much. It was not too long before Earl moved in with us at the Wolkengasse and became part of the family.

By that time I had pretty much given up on Heinz ever coming home and started the long bureaucratic process of having him declared dead.

While my parents loved Earl, we had some grief from the neighbors and the American authorities about our relationship. Not all Germans welcomed the Americans. "Ami, Go Home," was regularly sprayed on whatever concrete canvas remained in Giessen. Neighbors in the Wolkengasse warned me that there could be no permanent life with Earl. He would go back home and forget me. If he did take me to America, I should not be surprised that things were not as rosy as portrayed by many. The American authorities also did not condone relationships between Americans and Germans. There was an official anti-fraternization policy, although it was widely ignored. One day, when Earl and I were walking down the street with his arm around me, the military police (MPs) stopped us and let us know that touching between Americans and Germans was not allowed. In those first years after the war, marriage between Germans and Americans was also not allowed. After a while, the American Command gave up its anti-fraternization policies recognizing they could not go against human nature.

I had my anxious moments about Earl. I knew he was married but trusted him when he told me the marriage was over, and he would get a divorce as soon as possible. Still I worried. Would his mother and sisters accept me? When in 1951 Earl returned to the States for the funeral of his sister, Bernice, I wondered if he would return. When he did, I felt a lot more secure. I loved Earl and was prepared to trust and follow him anywhere.

It wasn't just his new family in the Wolkengasse that Earl enjoyed. He had grown up with and loved hunting with dogs on the Iowa prairies. We had room for dogs in our barn, and it wasn't long before Earl came home with his first dog. He was a big black hunting dog, named, Jacko. He looked fierce but was gentle with the family and especially attached to little Renate.

It was a cause for great amusement in the Wolkengasse that Renate and Jacko, looking like little Red Riding Hood and the wolf, went shopping together. On a daily basis, my mother would send them down the street to get bread. Jacko would make sure that Renate did not wander into the street. The money that my mother gave Renate to buy bread was safe because Jacko would have ripped the arm off anyone who approached her. I have fond memories of that very loyal and beautiful dog.

Jacko also had his wild side. One night, as American MPs walked by, they ran their billy clubs against the 6-foot-high gate that guarded the yard next to the house. Jacko lunged at the fence. The MPs shot him. Jacko lived but was never the same after that, and eventually we had him put down.

After Jacko came a series of German shepherds. How precious these dogs were to us can been seen in the many photos we had taken with the dogs. The last shepherd, Reif, came with us from Germany when we left in 1953.

Renate and our two shepherds, Alex and Baerbel, 1947

Me and two of our beloved Shepherds, Alex and Baerbel

In April 1949, Earl and I had a baby girl named Elda. As with Renate, I worked until the day of the birth. Both Renate and Elda were born in the *Wolkengasse* with Frau Sauter, the midwife who lived across the street, in attendance. They were both easy births. When Elda was born, I hardly went into labor. I had one big contraction, and there she was.

Renate 8 and Elda 1

We now had six adults and two children living in the four-room apartment in the Wolkengasse. There was my father and mother, Earl and me, and my younger brothers, Adolf and Albert. At some point, Albert's girlfriend, a refugee from Romania, named Hilde, also came to live with us. It wasn't too long until Albert and Hilde also had a baby, Erika. Our spacious apartment started to feel a little crowded.

When Earl was transferred from Giessen to Fulda, I decided to take Elda and rent a room near the army base. At that time, we also got our first car. Before we could settle in, Earl had a terrible car accident. Driving too fast one night, he came around a curve on a back road and hit a huge oak tree. The car was demolished. That Earl survived was a miracle. He had broken bones and swallowed a lot of glass that forever gave his voice a raspy edge, but otherwise he was completely recovered in a few weeks.

By 1953, a transfer back to the States seemed imminent. His divorce was final, but we had not received permission from the American authorities to marry. In my first marriage to Heinz Wessolek, I had to prove that I had no Jewish blood in me. This time, I had to prove I was not a communist. Investigators of the U.S. Occupation apparently had determined that our family had friends with communist connections.

We never knew who these friends were supposed to be. We guessed it might have been the Leuning family. Fritz Leuning had been friends and neighbors of my parents forever. Their sons and I grew up together on the Wolkengasse and spent countless hours together. If they were communists, we didn't know it. If we did know it, why would we care? Our families depended on each other. We worked hard. We cared about the children and about each other. We did the right things as we were told. The world of politics did not interest us.

Eventually, we overcame the objections of the American authorities and permission to marry was finally granted. On August 8, 1953, we married in the *Johannes Kirche*, one of the few churches to survive the war. It was the largest Lutheran church in Giessen

and an imposing monument to the power of the Lutheran religion in
Giessen.

The *Johanneskirche* in Giessen survived the war.
Earl and I were married there and generations
of the Marx family had their baptisms, confirmations,
marriages and funerals there.

Earl and I get married, August, 1953

Earl left soon after the wedding. I had to wait to follow him until we got orders and airplane tickets. In the meantime, I had to decide if Renate would go with me and Elda to the States or stay in Germany with my parents.

Earl and I in August 1953

Renate was 10 years old. She was a German girl who knew no English. My mother had raised her. They were extremely close. Others had left their German children behind when they followed their American husbands to the United States. My mother was distraught, but I felt Renate should go with me. Germany was still a poor country in 1953. Who knew what would happen? I thought she would have a better chance in life in the unknown country of America.

Renate

Cigarettes had an important role in both World War I and II. The entire military, no matter which side they fought on, were given cigarettes as a kind of psychological comfort and a form of currency. For Americans, cigarettes were included in the K-Rations. Extra cigarettes became a good source of income. As early as World War I, the military was targeted by tobacco companies, who promoted the use of cigarettes as a way for soldiers to escape from their current stress and to boost overall troop morale.

The Germans were in terrible distress in those first years after the war. The country was divided into two - East Germany and West Germany. In both the East and the West, cities lay in ruins, and 4.3 million military plus an additional 3 million or more civilians were dead. Disease and starvation plagued the civilian population. My mother's cousin, Lottie, died of tuberculosis, and I was a sickly child.

At the beginning of the occupation, there were strict laws about fraternizing with Germans. It didn't take too many months, however, before the authorities quit trying to enforce these laws. Many young men far from home and many young women without men and a need for food were a force more powerful than a military could command.

Wisely, the American authorities mostly ignored the fraternizing of Germans and Americans. Thousands of German women would marry Americans and move to the U.S.A.

In the United States, Congress was debating the future of Germany and Germans. Many of those in positions of power were of the opinion that because Germany was responsible for starting two world wars, it should never again become an industrial power. "Tear down their factories and let the Germans starve," they said, "so they can never be a threat again." Thank goodness for churches like the one in Hackensack, New Jersey, where ordinary citizens did what they could to help.

As the debate raged, it became more and more obvious to the USA, Great Britain, and France, that the real threat to the Allies came not from the Germans but from the Soviets. As soon as the war was over, the Allies and Soviets began to regard each other with suspicion. As early as March 1946, Winston Churchill warned the West that "an iron curtain has descended across the continent." The term symbolized efforts by the Soviet Union to block itself and its satellite states from open contact with the West and non-Soviet-controlled areas. On the East side of the Iron Curtain were the countries that were connected to or influenced by the Soviet Union. The "iron curtain," defined politics in the East and West until 1991 when the Berlin wall fell and Germany was unified again. I never expected to see Germany re-united in my lifetime. I was thrilled to watch thousands of ordinary Germans from the East and the West tear down the Berlin Wall stone by stone. A few later I had the pleasure of traveling in the former East Germany visiting many of the sites familiar to me through my studies of German literature and history.

By 1948, the Americans decided that rebuilding West Germany was the best way to deal with the threat of the Soviet Union. With the Marshall Plan, $17 billion (more than $160 billion in current dollar value) in American aid began to pour into West Germany, and Germany once again began to prosper. Today, a united Germany is a flourishing democracy and the biggest economic power in Europe.

CHAPTER 7

Coming to America
1953 to 2015

Lydia

On a cold, drizzly November 11, 1953, Renate, Elda and I got on an American military plane to leave our life in Germany forever. A couple of days earlier in Giessen, we had said our sad goodbyes. Would I ever see my parents and my brothers, Adolf and Albert, again? What would await me in a strange new country? Would my children and I be accepted by Earl's family? What about other Americans? Would they accept us? I was 28 years old and leaving the only life I had ever known for something completely unknown.

Yet, I was not afraid. I trusted Earl and my good luck that everything would turn out ok. Things were getting better in Germany, but life was still hard, and I hoped for a better future for myself and my children. I especially hoped that, in the United States, my children could fulfill my own ambition for a higher education.

There were about 50 passengers on the plane. They were all like me, wives of American soldiers and their children.

We had to travel the 4,500 miles on a propeller plane with few comforts. The trip itself took 35 hours. We flew from Frankfurt to Ireland, where we landed to refuel. From Ireland it was on to Iceland, where we refueled again before the nine- hour trip crossing the North Atlantic. Our next stop was a very cold and barren New- Foundland. We had a six-hour layover there. We got some food and had time to stretch our legs in the sparse military airport. Next came New York City.

Renate did not take well to air travel. She got sick almost immediately and vomited almost all the way from Frankfurt to New York. In those days, all airport seat pockets had those white plastic-coated bags for those who did not do well in the jockeying to and fro and, up and down, of a plane riding the currents of the air. She used at least a dozen bags and was not a happy camper.

At age four, Elda was a dynamo full of energy. She was a German Shirley Temple, very cute with brown curly hair and a flair for entertainment. She was everywhere, talking the whole time. Today, her six-year old grandson, Johnny, reminds me very much of Elda at that age. For me, the trip was exhausting.

We arrived in New York with three different passports. Elda was an American citizen. I had special status as the wife of an American but not a citizen, and Renate was a German citizen. At the end of that long journey, we had to go through immigration as three different citizens. It almost pushed me over the edge, but somehow, someway, I survived.

Arriving in New York in the middle of the night, we were led from the plane to two busses, which took us for a long two-hour drive to Fort Kilmer in New Jersey. There was not much assistance for mothers with young children. As the bus was ready to leave, I noticed that my bags still stood on the sidewalk. I got off the bus and asked for help putting the bags on the bus. I was asked to pay for such a service. When I offered all the change I had, I was told it was not enough. "Good, I said, "I will put the bags on the bus myself." And that is what I did.

To make matters worse, I was not sure where I was supposed to connect with Earl. I thought I would see him when we arrived in New York. But he was not there. After a phone call, I realized that Earl was expecting us to fly from New York to Chicago, where he would meet us and take us on the next stage of our journey. On my own, I had to figure out how to get airline tickets and how to travel from Fort Kilmer to the airport and on to Chicago. I don't know how I ever figured it out. All the German wives who came on that transport plane had to figure out how to get to their husbands. The military bureaucracy we had to deal with was polite but not very helpful. I had survived World War II, I thought, surely I could make it through this difficulty.

Once we arrived at Fort Kilmer, we were housed in military barracks with bunk beds, green scratchy green army blankets, and bars on the windows. I was upset about the bars on the windows, but I was too tired to protest. Early the next morning, we were roused from our unhospitable surroundings to figure out how to make the rest of the journey to Chicago, where we would be met by Earl and his family. Again, I don't know how I figured it out, but by afternoon we were back in New York ready to board a flight to Chicago.

The transport from New York to Chicago was non-military on American Airlines. It was a different experience from what we had just been through. In those days flight was still a luxury, and all passengers were treated with great care and comfort. Renate stopped vomiting. The stewardesses (yes, they were all very attractive women dressed in designer uniforms) made a fuss over me and the two children and made sure all our needs were met.

Still, I continued to be upset about my first night in America. When we arrived in Chicago, and I fell into Earl's arms after more than three days of travel, I told him I was ready to go back home to Germany. If I had really insisted, I think he would have arranged it. As it was, the worst was over and the best was yet to come. Earl's brother-in-law, Ted, told me that the whole family had been cooking for days to prepare for our arrival, and I had to go with them to meet the family.

Earl's mother and his sisters and brother-in-law were the most welcoming, kind and wonderful relatives one could ever imagine. They embraced my children and me with open arms. They did everything they could to make us feel comfortable and at-home in Clinton, Iowa, our first destination. For the rest of our lives, we were very close. Earl, his mother, and sisters all died before me, but I will never forget their kindness and their loving spirit.

After the holidays, it was time to transfer to Earl's new job as advisor to the National Guard in Pierre, South Dakota. Imagine the fertile place that was my home in Germany – flowing rivers and green rolling hills, a temperate climate, a tradition and culture more than one thousand years old. Pierre, South Dakota, on the other hand, was a dry, desolate plain. Less than 75 years before, it had been Indian territory, controlled by the Sioux warrior tribe. South Dakota had rattlesnakes that could hide in a downtown location to strike at the unaware passer-by. There were warnings about tornados, which could suddenly dip down from the sky destroying everything in their path. There were animals and birds I had never seen or even heard of – buffaloes and long-horn steer, pheasants and grouse. Just a few blocks from our first home in Pierre, there was an Indian Reservation, where it was said they ate dogs. In the summer it was blazing hot and in the winter blizzards would blow across the empty prairie and cover our house to the roof.

Renate(12) and Elda(6) in Pierre, SD

Still, the people were very kind and helpful. Earl was able to pursue his favorite sport of hunting, and we enjoyed many a tasty pheasant at the dinner table. Renate and Elda loved the beautiful colorful feathers.

Earl's salary supported a very modest lifestyle. We lived from paycheck to paycheck. We bought a refrigerator on credit, but I did not think I needed to go into debt for a washer and dryer. I washed our laundry in the bathtub and hung the laundry outside to dry. This worked well in the summer, but in the winter sheets and cotton diapers froze on the line. When they thawed out, I ironed them. It was a lot of trouble, but there was no sweeter smell than sheets and laundry dried in the South Dakota sunshine.

I worked hard to maintain the household, but I got homesick, especially when Earl had to travel to other National Guard bases in the rest of the state. I missed the trees, and I would have given anything for some substantial German bread. The soft white stuff that passed for bread in America was not to my liking. Eventually I learned that the local hospital was run by German nuns. When I was lonely, I would go and talk to them in German. The Mother Superior suggested that, to be less lonely, I should get a job. I was all in favor of that, and we really needed the money, but I didn't know what I could do.

When she learned I had been a bookkeeper in Germany, she hired me on the spot. The hospital had just bought the latest technology in bookkeeping and needed someone to learn how to operate it. I learned the new bookkeeping machine and did the billing at night. I also learned how to operate the switchboard phone system. When the switchboard and bookkeeping did not take all my time at night, I was expected to feed the new babies. I loved my job. We had extra income and I was at the start of a wonderful career that I could never have dreamed of in Germany.

While we lived in South Dakota, I became an American citizen. Wives of Americans could apply for citizenship after three years of living in the country and showing that they could read, write and speak English. To help prepare me, the U.S. government gave me some books on U.S. history. Renate and I studied these texts together. Maybe that was the beginning of her love of history.

In 1956, I applied for citizenship and appeared before a local judge. He asked me a few questions and the Mother Superior from the hospital testified that I was an excellent candidate for citizenship. I didn't know what to do about Renate and told the judge that when she was older she should decide for herself whether or not she wanted to be an American citizen. The judge convinced me that as an American citizen Renate would have many advantages that she might not have as a German. In the end, Renate became an American citizen as part of the same ceremony.

Earl and I had two more children, Ronald (1955) and Barbara (1957.) We were transferred from South Dakota to Fort Ord, California, on the beautiful Monterey Peninsula. We bought a home in Pacific Grove, California. I had a successful career in the development of the Community Hospital of the Monterey Peninsula (CHOMP). We raised a family and sent two children to college, the first in the family to have a higher education. Earl died as a result of lung cancer in 1992. My children have flourished and had more children. I now have eight grandchildren and twelve great-grandchildren. In March, 2015, I had my first great-great-grandchild.

My 30 years at CHOMP gave me many opportunities that had been denied to me in Germany. The hospital administrator, Mr. Tom Tonkin, was an extraordinary manager and great human being. He recognized my ambition and talent and gave me every opportunity I was willing to take. From being a bookkeeper and switchboard operator, I became a manager of the financial office of CHOMP. During my career at CHOMP, we built a beautiful new hospital, learned the rules of the new federal Medicare and Medicaid programs, and moved into the computer age. Together with Mr. Tonkin, I welcomed delegates from the German parliament, who wanted to see the innovations in our hospital. Over the years, I had the chance to talk with Clint Eastwood, Doris Day, and other Hollywood stars who made their home on the Monterey Peninsula. I loved my years at CHOMP. Working there was a total dream. If I had to do it over again I would not change anything.

Ten years after I left Germany, I made my first trip back. In February, 1963, my brother Adolf sent a telegram saying that if I wanted to see my father again, I would have to come right away. I borrowed the money for the plane ticket and a couple of days later left for Germany. After I arrived, my father lived for three more days. He died at age 60 of stomach cancer. It was a difficult trip. I was afraid of the long flight, worried about my children at home and grieved with my mother and brothers at the untimely death of my father.

My mother, brothers, and I in the 1960s

After that trip, however, it was clear to me that while I hoped for many more family visits, I was never going back to Germany permanently. My mother came twice to California and stayed for six months each time. I wanted her to stay permanently, but her roots were planted too deep in German soil to move permanently to Monterey. My brother, Adolf and his wife Irmgard, came several times and other German relatives and friends came to visit and enjoy the extraordinary California Central Coast. With modern technology, keeping in touch with people half a world away is not as difficult as when we first came in 1953. It has taken some effort, but I kept my feet planted in both worlds, one in old Germany and one in the beautiful and amazing state of California.

I am 90 years old this year. Who could imagine a greater journey than from Nazi Germany and World War II to the peaceful little paradise of Pacific Grove, California.

Me and my four children in 1992
From left to right: Renate, Barbara, Ron, Elda

Printed in the United States
By Bookmasters